Ernest Campbell

Experimental
Preaching

Experimental Preaching

edited by
John Killinger

ABINGDON PRESS
Nashville and New York

Library of Congress Cataloging in Publication Data

KILLINGER, JOHN, comp. Experimental preaching.
CONTENTS: Shehorn, D. I want to see God.—Martin, T. B. 2001: the church revisited.—Denham, A. A freedom sermon. [etc.]
1. Sermons, American. 2. Preaching. I. Title.
BV4241.K48   252   72-8419

ISBN 0-687-12423-9

MANUFACTURED BY THE PARTHENON PRESS AT
NASHVILLE, TENNESSEE, UNITED STATES OF AMERICA

FOR ZEUS
*who would probably enjoy this
if he could read it*

Contents

Introduction

The words "experimental preaching" suggest that it is a new kind of preaching. Actually it is and it isn't. It plays its part in the effervescence of modern life. But there has always been an experimentalism at work among authentic preachers.

The central problem which all speakers face, of having something significant to say and discovering forms of discourse to shape the communication of that something, has fostered a spirit of inventiveness in every age. Socrates' questions, Jeremiah's symbolic acts, Jesus' parables, Origen's biblical exposition, Luther's *methodus heroica*, the long, hypnosis-inducing sermons of the Puritans and frontier evangelists—there was something new and different about each of these methods.

The only rule is that there are no rules which may not be broken. Real communication is not static and can seldom be accomplished for very long without experimentation and innovation. The business of mediating reality and effecting orderly perception out of a chaos of possibilities requires constant probing for new means and techniques.

It is unfortunately true that most of the sermons

9

heard by most of the congregations in Christendom have nothing at all new about them. They belong to the calendar variety of art—the usual subjects drawn off in the customary style to produce the standard result. There have been some superb artisans in the calendar idiom through the years—Norman Rockwells of the pulpit who have never ceased to charm and delight their audiences. And by far the majority of people in the world obviously prefer calendar reproductions to the best of the Dadaist or expressionist painters. Otherwise one would not experience such a delicious sense of space and aloneness on a weekday in the Musée de l'Art Moderne, and these evanescent, privately printed little magazines of the arts would not disappear after three or four issues but would grow slick and bloated on public consumption.

But perhaps this is not to be lamented. Inertia may be as important a quality in the physics of the mind as it is in the physics of the universe. I have several conservative friends for whose stabilizing influence I am often grateful. I can always find them in the dark—they have not moved far from where they were the last time. They afford a measure of comfort in the era of implosion and future shock. I can always count on them not to understand.

Still, it is impossible to overestimate the importance of the new in either the arts or religion. Imagine the stagnation of the human sensibilities without it. Life would become all *method*, as Nietzsche complained, with nothing to do but reproduce the same thoughts and images in ever greater detail and expertise. The technicians would rule everything in a growing tyranny of fineness and exactitude. The spirit of man, like the delicate song of a bird, would be muffled forever under successive layers of "improvements."

The Likelihood of Idolatry

It would be especially wrong in religion not to encourage newness. What is heard too long or seen too long or felt too long in the same manner inevitably becomes idolatrous. It is first *associated* with the object of worship. Then it becomes *identified* and *confused* with the object of worship. And it ends, in most cases, by *supplanting* the object of worship. This is of course why Calvin inveighed so vehemently against iconography of any kind in the sanctuary, insisting on whitewashed walls adorned only, on occasion, by texts from sacred scripture. Despite this sweeping rejection of visible images so liable to become religious fixations to the worshipers, however, he showed little awareness of the way in which verbal images or icons likewise subvert men's loyalties, or of the way in which even the idiom of severity and plainness can beguile the mind into standardized responses and ways of thinking. Given the manner in which human perception and human knowing function, there is only one true alternative to idolatry, and that is the induction of a constant state of change and disorientation, so that the mind must strive constantly to reperceive and reknow the object of devotion otherwise taken for granted.

We resist instinctively the discomfort of this unsettled condition, preferring always the security of some opinion already established or agreed upon. T. S. Eliot snapped our family portrait in these lines from *The Family Reunion*:

> Why do we all behave as if the door might
>   suddenly open, the curtains be drawn,
> The cellar make some dreadful disclosure,
>   the roof disappear,
> And we should cease to be sure of what is
>   real or unreal?
> Hold tight, hold tight, we must insist that
>   the world is what we have always taken
>   it to be.[1]

Most of us want the world to be what we have always taken it to be. Some of us will even fight for the assurance that it is. And that means that God must be what we have always taken him to be. And salvation and sin and holiness and spirituality and death and life after death and all the rest. It is easier to change everything than it is to change one or two items and then hold the rest where they are. So, not wanting to wake up like spiritual Rip Van Winkles in an entirely new soulscape, we oppose all change and evolution. The deity we worship, no longer known in the static discharge which once occurred as we entered the vale of discovery, becomes an idol—the ossification of a once-upon-a-time experience.

Language as Probe

Martin Heidegger, in his book *On the Way to Language*, offers an interesting phenomenological account of how words and thoughts function. The mystery of language is such, he suggests, that we begin to experience it at its highest only when we cease to treat it as an instrument or a tool and follow in its way. Our culture

1. *The Family Reunion*, in *The Complete Poems and Plays, 1909-1950*; by permission of Harcourt Brace Jovanovich and Faber and Faber Ltd.

has become so utilitarian that we tend to regard words as a means to an end. The "way"—what the Chinese philosopher Lao-tzu called the *tao*—is superficially thought of as "a stretch connecting two places." We use language, therefore, merely to reach certain goals which we already had in mind when we began. We don't permit it to unfold as we go, to lead us along paths where knowledge is uncertain, revealing new worlds to us in the process.[2]

This has exciting implications, it seems to me, for religious speech. It helps to restore a sense of wonderment to the entire business of speaking about God. Sermons which know where they are going, because they have been there so many times before, are no sermons at all. The object which they propose to reach is laid down ahead of time and the phrases—clichés, this makes them —set end to end to attain it. The sermon is built like a highway—an *interstate* highway—instead of like a tenuous path in the wilderness. The saying of Jesus blares at us again: *narrow* is the way that leads to life.

Seriousness is part of our bane. We are so dreadfully prosaic about spiritual things. What began in one generation as poetry—rhythmical, playful, witty (all adjectives constituent of the matrix of invention or discovery)—became the sodden, sullen, heavy prose of successive times. The fire was damped and banked and nearly smothered. Angels ceased to come. Devils were seen no more. Committees took over where artists and madmen had left off, the breath hardly cold in their lungs.

Kierkegaard in his satirical writings and Freud in his essay on "Wit and the Unconscious" pioneered the view

2. *On the Way to Language*, trans. Peter D. Hertz (New York: Harper and Row, 1971), esp. pp. 91-93.

that the greatest creativity is often linked to a sense of playfulness. André Breton and the early surrealists arrived independently at the same opinion and encouraged a zaniness in their circles which is now being reassessed by critics as a ground for immensely significant contributions to the arts in the past half century. Arthur Koestler, in his monumental study *The Act of Creation*, identifies humor as the quality of spirit which breaks the circuits of habit in the human mind and enables originality and discovery to occur.[3]

All of this is related to what Heidegger says about the open-endedness of language. The playful spirit is committed to the game, not to the end in view. It is humble enough, self-emptied enough, to be led or seduced by the currents of the play. It does not manifest high control needs, but abandons itself to the activity and to whatever outcome eventuates.

The religious mind has all too often been a closed mind. It tends to accept uncritically the doctrines and dogmas recommended by cultic leaders, unmindful of the grossly human and secular conditions under which the teachings originally took shape. Then it automatically rules out all other possibilities and spends its energies trying to force all new experiences and acquisitions of knowledge into conformity with the doctrinal position. True novelty is completely ruled out. Method or technique is the only variable permitted, and even that is kept at a low grade lest it threaten a reformulation of the dogmas.

Several of the examples of experimental preaching in this collection were included because of their playfulness

3. *The Act of Creation: A Study of the Conscious and Unconscious in Science and Art* (New York: Dell Publishing Co., 1964), pp. 44-45.

14

and their authors' willingness to grant enough freedom to method to make possible a subversion of doctrine. It may be complained by the conservative reader that they go too far and in some instances actually alter the original message of Christianity. Such a reader will probably say that he does not find the *kerygma*, the storied framework of the early church, shining through luminously enough, casting its beneficent light on our nocturnal landscapes. But that is to commit the religious fallacy which is the error even of classical Christian thought—namely, of focusing too closely and carefully on the various *particulars* of the *kerygma* and missing the total pattern or gestalt, which says that man is a free spirit and must not be indentured to any system.

This, then, is the primary theological assumption underlying the assembling of the pieces in this book: God, in Christ, has called us out from all totalitarian superstructures, even those of the mind and spirit, and it is wrong of us to obligate or enslave ourselves to them again, even in the name of religion and piety. Our first obligation now is to our own centers of freedom.

Eugene O'Neill had the matter more by the tail in his play *Lazarus Laughed* than I used to realize, when he characterized the resurrection of Lazarus as essentially a restoration to Dionysian freedom and laughter. He had one player describe the parting of Jesus and Lazarus after the miracle this way:

> And then Lazarus knelt and kissed Jesus' feet and both of them smiled and Jesus blessed him and called him 'My Brother' and went away; and Lazarus, looking after Him, began to laugh softly like a man in love with God! Such a laugh I never heard! It made my ears drunk! It was like

15

wine! And though I was half-dead with fright I found myself laughing, too! [4]

The house of Lazarus in Bethany became known as the "House of Laughter." The spirit of freedom which issues in laughter transcends all systems and categorizations, refuses them as a hare refuses the briar patch, darting here and there among them, having advantage of them, but denying them as final arbiters of his mode of life and thought. As Paul himself wrote, "We have not received again the spirit of bondage."

This is the significance of the title of Harold Bales's sermon at the end of the anthology, "You Can't Nail Jesus Down." Its irony suggests an important truth. We are fully as unsuccessful in pinning Jesus down with our pieties and theologies as the Roman garrison in Jerusalem was in confining his influence at the place of crucifixion.

What has been called the *kenosis* or self-emptying of Christ finally makes it impossible for us to make any unambiguous statements about him. Who he was, what he did, what he meant by what he said, has a way of eluding us. Precisely when we think we have caught the truth in our hands and call to a neighbor to look, it evaporates and leaves us feeling silly and empty-handed. What is asked for is a spirit of constant inquiry—a pledge to follow in the way without either the hope or the despair of arriving at finalities.

Jesus *taunts* us to come after him, and we are away on a game of Follow the Leader. The game alone permits us to escape the perennial tyrannies of time, space, and conclusion.

4. *Lazarus Laughed*, in *Nine Plays by Eugene O'Neill* (New York: Modern Library, n.d.), p. 385.

A *Great Time for Preaching*

Speaking of time, this is a propitious moment for preachers to throw off the bondage of homiletical traditions grown fat and sassy like mistresses too sure of themselves. Experimentalism is in the air everywhere. Consider the names of even a minor catalog of artists, thinkers, and doers at work in the United States today: Cage, Sessions, Kubrick, Oldenburg, McLuhan, Fuller, Brautigan, Burroughs, Blau, Mailer, Hansen, Bernstein. A yeasty ferment is at work in almost every area of human existence. Habits of thought are being exploded daily. Walls of tradition are brought tumbling down. Slaves are in a panic—their whole world is collapsing. Free men exult—a new world is being born.

A further condition favorable to experimentation is the chaotic state of formal criticism in almost every field. Dame Helen Gardner, Merton Professor of English Literature at Oxford University, said in a recent book on tragedy that the conspicuous weakness and confusion of critical theories in Elizabethan times, combined with a variety of dramatic forms and conventions, gave Shakespeare almost total freedom as an artist to follow wherever his fecund imagination led him, and surely account in significant measure for the brilliance of his achievement.[5] The same situation exists for the contemporary preacher. A profusion of homiletical theory is now pouring forth, but without consensus. The secure old positions and rationales of Broadus and Sangster no longer cast their freezing shadows over neophyte preachers—the former are indeed almost unknown among the latter.

5. Helen Gardner, *Religion and Literature* (New York: Oxford University Press, 1971), p. 68.

Ivan Karamazov said that when God is dead everything is permitted. Now that the pseudodeity of more than a millennium of stultifying orthodoxy is dead (his carcass is not entirely out of the way in many churches), everything is permitted in the sermon. The explosion of form itself signals a new health and vitality in the general spiritual enterprise.

In this interregnum of dethroned criticism, art has become suspect. Too frequently, say the radical young artists, it has been identified almost solely as technical efficiency, as expertise in method and execution. Examples of this debased understanding of true art, they insist, are mere "garbage," crystallizations and extensions of the mass mind.

Real art involves exploration and discovery. It may not even involve permanency, as the old *vita breva, ars longa* formula had it, but may be as fleeting and perishable as a moment of recognition. The true artist, then, never worships at the shrine of what he has done. He is always in flight, always on the way, risking himself again and again for the disclosures by which he sustains his spirit.

He refuses the former aesthetic considerations in favor of shock and immediacy. "Beauty is almost no longer possible if it is not a lie," says R. D. Laing.[6] "I must write and tell him [a friend] about beauty," says John Cage, "the urgency to avoid it." [7] Beauty was a form of societal enslavement which did not translate well from

6. R. D. Laing, *The Politics of Experience* (New York: Ballantine Books, 1967), p. 11.
7. John Cage, *A Year from Monday* (Middletown, Conn.: Wesleyan University Press, 1969), p. 12.

one culture to another and is therefore being transcended now by a kind of global panculturalism. The communication of a work of art is less rigged or controlled in this new situation. It is allowed to happen, to evoke whatever meanings it will in the person "participating" in the work or becoming involved with it. The mind is freed for new possibilities.

This kind of trust is aimed at in many of the sermons in this anthology. They too refuse the classical traditions of beauty and greatness. While they are often imaginatively conceived and dashed off with piquancy or élan, they retain a sense of disposability, as though they were composed for immediate consumption and not as objects to be plasticized in the pages of a book of great sermons. Some of them are plainly abrasive, screaming out their points in order to be heard and reacted against. They indicate the recognition on the part of their authors that the communication of the gospel of Jesus is not something to be accomplished in a single, blinding flash of the strobe, but is picked up prismatically and mirrored in a constantly rotating field of flecks and pieces—that it is a process not centripetal but centrifugal, infinitely expansive in all directions, a cosmos with an inexhaustible supply of stars.

They reflect the opinion which John Fry sets down in his inimitable James Cagney inimitable rhetoric, that:

Great preaching is just no longer appropriate. For the principal reason that there are so few great churches in which the great preaching can be done. The classical great sermon in a less than, or no longer, great church is worse than inappropriate. It is an anachronism. An irrelevance. Like a Lyceum lecture at a go-go palace or a Klan rally. I mean, one of those beautiful sermons—three points, amply and aptly illustrated, solid, and Biblical, constructed in style suitable for sending to *Harper's* on Monday morning—these sermons have got to have beautiful churches full of people who might discreetly note a minor syntactical lapse. And that is the kind of church we are fresh out of. The presence of national issues has forced a reconsideration of the whole matter of greatness. A big church which makes a mighty witness is great by the *new* terms of greatness, as is the little church which hangs in there, even if a spider now and again can be discerned crawling around on a pew. The new terms of greatness come from action in response to these issues, not because of brilliant preaching. In fact, great preaching—in that fine old three-solid-points-and-lots-of-stories tradition—to a white-power bunch becomes anti-great, as well as grotesque. Aspiring to great preaching in that same white-power situation is ridiculous. The greater the words, the more greatly they mock preacher and hearers alike if they do not well up from within a situation of action.[8]

It is a good time to be a preacher, as it is a good time to be an artist. The weight of the centuries is off us. We don't have to reperform the whole history of preaching or the whole history of art in what we do now. We don't have to out-Titian Titian or out-Rembrandt Rembrandt or out-Chrysostom Chrysostom or out-Luther Luther. All we have to do is to react honestly, simply, humanly to what is around us on the basis of whatever we bring to the occasion. The pressure is gone. It will build again, and history will sit like a stone on our groins again, but for the moment we are free. It is a time for fireworks, a time for chuckles and chortles, a time for breathing.

8. John Fry, *Fire and Blackstone* (Philadelphia: J. B. Lippincott Co., 1969), pp. 22-23.

The Problem with "Printing" Experimental Sermons and a Word About Media

Of course many of these disposable sermons, if not all of them, have suffered in translation to the printed page. A sermon is actually a happening, like a dinner party or a game or a birthday celebration. It cannot be "caught" by a secretary or a tape recorder—at least, not in its essential nature. A good reporter might catch some of the flavor of it by describing not only the sermon but how the preacher and the congregation interacted with it. Even then much would be lost. The flesh-and-blood sermon is multidimensional, the printed sermon one-dimensional or less.

This observation is doubly or triply true of experimental sermons. Because they depend more on novelty and less on linear exposition than traditional sermons, the interface with the congregation is especially important. Sixteen video-tape sound cameras, aimed from all levels and directions, would be required to *begin* to record congregational portraits of some of the sermons in this book.

A book, moreover, is confined to a more-or-less linear approach even in a reporter's description of a sermon. Yet many of the sermons within these covers were designed for use with various multimedia effects, such as lights, films, music, props, and physical movement. And other sermons which really ought to be involved in any consideration of experimental preaching simply could not be included because they were so completely nonlinear as to defy bibliomentation.

This is a shortcoming of the anthology, and I apologize for it. I simply did not know how to adequately overcome it. I have attempted, in three or four cases, to provide enough documentation to make the sermons comprehensible even though their life-contexts or ecologies could never be reduced to paper. But it can only be hoped that the reader has had his own experiences in congregational settings where the sermon was primarily nonlinear and can realize how far toward the linear end of the spectrum these particular sermons really are.

I must take some consolation in the fact that the reader's imagination is a significant ingredient in the making of any book—an unknowable x-factor, as it were, which will from time to time catch fire and burn with that gemlike flame, pure, serene, which renders the printed page inconsequential while creativity flashes out. For what is important, in the end, is not the acceptance or rejection of this material, but whether it succeeds in sparking ideas and projects in the reader's own combustion chambers.

The imaginative preacher, once he is impressed by the notion that a sermon can transcend the old linear models, will have little trouble improvising the tools and techniques required to do his own thing. He doesn't need a thousand dollars worth of camera and sound equipment to mount multimedia sermons in his church. Improvising is "in" these days, and slickness is out. Improvisation conveys the personality of the improvisor; professionalism doesn't. And personality is valued.

A great slide show can be produced with a fifty-dollar camera, a few dollars worth of film commercially processed, and a bedsheet hung in the chancel. Marvelous sound effects can be obtained with two or three inexpensive tape recorders placed around the sanctuary, or with a few volunteers playing instruments or manipulating homemade noise boxes. Television sets, garden tools, children's toys, old bedsprings, buggy whips—anything can become an implement when used with imagination. Remember, this is the age which began with Marcel Duchamp's exhibit of a urinal in an art show with the sign "Fountain" over it and which features a play by Fernando Arrabal in which the stage settings are comprised entirely of derelict automobile bodies from a wrecking yard! "Camp" is in and "plastic" is out.

Nor should it be overlooked that our physical bodies are also media and can be employed in sermons. The church has had a lingering phobia about the body, but that is beginning to be dissipated in some places. The emphasis today on psychosomatic health is fast making its way into theological consideration. In a seminar on experimental preaching and worship, my students have led us at various times in relaxation exercises, sensitivity training, free dance movement, and body painting. The effect has been to produce a sense of relationship among us that goes much deeper than mere verbal relationship. There is a feeling of corporateness underlying even our moments of verbal exchange, as though we could communicate by touch or movement if the words became ineffective.

Psychologists have observed that our skin gives us a false impression of isolation from the rest of the physical world. It appears to define us over and against the environment, when in fact it is only a loosely woven blanket of insulative material which "breathes" and facilitates our interaction with the ecosystem. We should learn to regard it as a *liquid* boundary through which we engage in constant interplay with our sustaining environment.

Letting the body communicate in worship by "speaking," exploring, feeling, "hearing," and participating in its environment was vital in every primitive religion. Now, after an interdiction of hundreds of years, the importance of this practice is being rediscovered. Ministers in our seminar sessions often express amazement after "lubrication" exercises; they didn't know they could feel so good, or that the body could become a part of preaching.

Education for Change

A word of advice is in order about the use of experimental methods in congregations that are substantially traditional and nonexperimental in their orientation.

People in the Western world are normally resistant to change or innovation. They have been taught from childhood that tradition, as Tevye says in *Fiddler on the Roof*, supports the whole world. Our entire system of education enforces such a notion. It is designed, as its critics remind us today, to induce stasis, not to encourage change.

And the church, far from being the D.E.W. line of culture which McLuhan claims that the artists are, is actually the Maginot Line—the line of last resort, where fortifications are thickest and trenches are deepest and desperations are highest. If the church gives way to the times, think many people, there is no ground to retreat to. The battle is lost. Therefore the line must be held. No price is too great. We must save the religion of our fathers!

(Actually, nobody in any age ever truly follows his father's religion, because, as Laing reminds us in *The Politics of Experience*, no one can ever experience an-

24

other person's experience—he can only experience the other person as the other person experiences it. But thinking we do assuages some of the guilt we bear subconsciously for having ever wished the deaths of our male parents or departed from their households.)

Before they ever hit their congregations bang in the eye with sudden changes in sermonic fare, ministers should expend some tactful effort toward reeducating them to the significance and positive value of change in their lives. Shocking them without warning is an ego trip for some ministers. But over the long haul people must be brought to see that novelty and change constitute the basis for stimulation and renewal, not, as they had probably thought, chaos and disaster. If they are really to be the people of God, that honorable and ancient designation of *laos tou theou*, then they must become involved firsthand in the rethinking and reconceptualization of the task and message of the church in our time. They have got to be makers and designers of change.

The task of reeducation may not be as hopeless as it sometimes seems. The public once regarded Marcel Duchamp, Salvador Dali, and Antonin Artaud as being radically and hopelessly insane. But appreciative critics eventually did their work of selling the public on the importance of new perspectives. Younger artists and playwrights grew up in the idiom of novelty and no longer found it strange. The whole world of the artist was transformed. It became commonplace to hear Picasso remark, "I often paint fakes," or "I lie in order to tell the truth."

It is the preacher's job, insofar as he is still interested in communicating within the brick-and-ivied structures of the church, to make the pulpit safe for experimentation. Not too safe, perhaps. There is an element of risk in

25

life that would be only inappropriately missing from the sermon. But the creative preacher will find ways of developing resonance in his congregation for what he is doing—little pockets or enclaves of those who are still intrigued enough to follow "in the way" and see where it leads them, who want to move up from partial play to full play in their religion, and who will applaud the difficult gambits which flirt with failure on the way to some minor successes in their behalf.

These persons may not be able to carry the vote when the congregation decides to reinvest its spiritual security and peace of mind with a soberer and more tradition-oriented broker. But they will surely be God's own comfort to a down-at-the-heels and out-on-his-can minister who loves to fondle his memories of how he once made religion real and exciting to a handful of people who were ready to throw in the towel because they couldn't stand the boredom any more!

I Want to See God

I want to see God now! I want to see God now!
                                    I want to. I want to.
I want
   want; want; want; want; want; want; want; want; want;;;;
      I . .
         I . . . . .
            I ah . . . .
               ah
                  nuthin.
I want to see God now!
   Gabriel's horn
      In the mouth of a babe.

Four years old and about three feet tall
   blond and blue-eyed.
      Close-cropped bangs swept a baby-faced brow.
         He stood clad in gray
            English cut—
               giving an air of royalty.

The Rev. Don Shehorn is minister of the Universal City Baptist Church, Universal City, Texas 74148.

The little viking stood hand on hip
intimidating me.
Innocent eyes peered through long
motionless lashes as He repeated
what I thought He had said.
"I want to see God now."

I know the terror of judgment.
He had stolen my lines.
But how does one answer a prayer?
Typical of my trade, I tried.
Taking advantage of his age
and my exalted station
muttered something about God
in Jesus. . .heaven. . .
and the world.

I avoided contact with evil
and good
without success.

Although a ballerina would have envied my
tippy-toeing through those tulips
my little Enemy wasn't impressed.
With a shrug of His shoulders
He walked away.
With His pink friend.

After He had retreated
I experienced that cold sweaty sensation
That often accompanies revelation.

28

The war wasn't over.
　　All day long I lived in a nightmare world.
　　　He kept coming back.
　　　　Each time with age
　　　　　the demand was phrased
　　　　　　in language universal.

He came back at six
　　at sixteen
　　　and sixty.

　　　　At six the hostility of the playground
　　　　　and the loneliness of overcrowded classroom
　　　　　had worn the cord.
　　　　　　The lines of confidence were yet there
　　　　　　but lines of doubt appeared
　　　　　　　when He thought Himself alone.

The age of the bland demand had passed.
　He squared His "manly" shoulders
　　grinned through gaps
　　　and made castles in sand.

Dismal castles
　falling before a regretful toe
　　framing the demand in sand
　　　"I want to see God now."

　　　　With trembling hand
　　　　I smoothed the sand
　　　　　lest His demand
　　　　　　cry out from the ground

29

like Abel's blood
and I stand
with red hands.

At sixteen the head bows
the beard browns
and hair falls around
stooped shoulders.

The would-be bride
a hide no longer pink
clutched His hand questioningly.
His Harley hog throws sand
and gravel and rubber
spending its life scribbling
"I want to see God now.

The sun having set at noon
circles behind dark clouds
of memory.

An occasional ray
reflected off a broken cloud
startles and blinds.
Shielding His eyes
He gropes for the door
of His dimly lit room.
Hesitantly, reluctantly, ineffectively
He fondles the knob.

With a sigh like ah
he proceeds through the door

stumping His toe on a piece of stripping
  too long nailed down.

Out of the heart of a child
  an honest question
    muffled through masks
      of time and place
        still alive
          in a reluctant hand
            and forgetful toe;
              wistfully reminiscent
                of a once bland demand.
                  "I want to see God now."

Gaps will close
  with gleaming ivory.
    Shoulders will stoop
      with time.
          The burden of an unheard demand
          lies buried in sand
          or borne by accident.

Echoing
  from the mouth of a babe
    like a trumpet!
    like a trumpet!
    like a trumpet!

"I want to see God now."
        Now!
        Now!
        Now!

31

Is He in the womb?
  Or the tomb?

            Has anyone seen Him lately?
            In a sandpile???
              On a motorcycle???
              In a shack???
                  In grave clothes???

2001:
The Church Revisited

The originator of this "science fiction" liturgy and sermon says that he has taken his clues "from the scientists and ecologists who predict great shortages of food, water, air, and power, rather than from the science fiction writers who see vast technological feats in the future, as per the movie *2001*. Presuppositions are that the congregation will be small and poor, that Christianity will be a minority religion, and that most adults will have poor health and one or more respiratory diseases and will need to wear breathing apparatus. As worship has not changed drastically over the past 300 years, I do not think the forms will change much in the average congregation in the next thirty years; but the meaning of worship will be markedly deepened in the face of severe hardships."

When the service is performed, participants wear plastic surgical masks which are inexpensive and obtainable at any medical supply store. At the time of communion the officiating minister elevates some plastic grapes on the table, to remind the worshipers that such fruits once grew on the earth, and a loaf of bread, now encased in plastic, to remind them of what hearth bread looked like. Now the bread is in the form of

The Rev. Thomas B. Martin is minister of Southminster Presbyterian Church, Nashville, Tennessee 37211.

miniature wafers (how many churches have already gone to this!), and the "wine" is made before the worshipers' eyes by pouring Kool-Aid powder into a flask of sterilized water. The high point of the service is reached as worshipers remove their surgical masks to take communion and *pass their breath* from one to another.

As the author suggests, the dislocation achieved by having a congregation act out a different situation and life-style from the one it is accustomed to helps immensely in discovering insights related to present situations and styles of worship.

The Church of the Remnant

April 26, 2001
Service of Worship

Call to Worship

 Minister: Let us worship God.

 People: Praise to you, O Lord our God, ruler of the universe, who causes the earth to support life for all creatures!

 All: Amen.

The Confession (Minister and People)

 Almighty God, in the past you have given us more than we needed or deserved, yet we always wanted more and more, and we refused to love your gifts of life. Now our earth is wasted, our air is poisoned, our water is polluted, and we resent what we lack. God, forgive our stubborn greed and our destructiveness. In mercy show us the way to cleanse, rebuild, and replant our world. Continue your covenant with us; through Jesus Christ our Lord. Amen.

The Sermon: "Insiders and Outsiders" (appended)

The Hymn: "Breathe on Me, Breath of God"

34

Breathe on me, Breath of God,
Fill me with life anew,
That I may love what thou dost love,
And do what thou wouldst do.

Breathe on me, breath of God,
Until my heart is pure,
Until with thee I will one will,
To do and to endure.

Breathe on me, breath of God,
So shall I never die,
But live with thee the perfect life
Of Thine eternity. Amen.

The Prayer of Thanksgiving (In Unison)

We praise you, God our creator, for your good gifts to us and all men. We thank you for the friendship of Christ and each other. We thank you for the promise of your coming kingdom, where there will be no gasping for breath, no gnawing hunger, no parched lips longing for clean water; where men and women will breathe the holy spirit and be filled to satisfaction by your love. We thank you for this precious loaf which reminds us that once grain was abundant and now is scarce; so, at one time Christians were abundant and are now a tiny minority. As we recall Christ and the precious few in the upper room, we find heart and the courage to continue. Amen.

The Communion

The Recognition—"And their eyes were opened and they recognized him."

(Remove breathing masks)

The Breath—"He then breathed on them."

The Bread—"This is my body."

35

The Wine—"This cup is the new covenant in my blood."

Closing Prayer and Benediction

Announcements:

The plastic flowers decorating our sanctuary are a gift of Ms. Mary Blue in memory of her husband, Robert Barnes, whose body was frozen in April, 1987.

Our future hope! Bill and Helen Brown-Smith have received authorization from the Population Control Board to have a child. Their geneticist assures them they will have a boy.

The Parks and Recreation Authority has promised us a deactivated 1979 Ford Pinto for our children's playground. This relic of the golden age of transportation when citizens were still allowed private vehicles was one of the last superluxury sedans having a 130-inch wheelbase and a 400-horsepower engine. It should be great fun for the children and serve as a reminder for all of us of our past materialism and wastefulness.

INSIDERS AND OUTSIDERS

Text: Ephesians 2:14 (RSV): "For he is our peace, who has made us both one, and has broken down the dividing wall of hostility."

Friends, again we gather to worship God and give thanks for the good life we enjoy. We are grateful that through God's grace we are among those who live under the Dome with its breathable air, controlled climate, and all the other marvels of technology that provide us with a reasonably wholesome environment.

There are those who find the necessity of wearing air filter masks inconvenient, and some of the older citizens still complain about the taste of manufactured food products, yet life is truly good in Domecile.

Unfortunately, things are not nearly so good outside the Dome. Most Domecilians have absolutely no idea how terrible it is on the outside. The Outsiders exist in the worst possible atmosphere. The air is as thick as pea soup—each breath filling their lungs with enough pollutants to put a Domecilian in the infirmary for a month. We would consider their water supply nonpotable, yet it is all they have, so they drink it. They live on a minimal diet of soybeans and seaweed. It is amazing that they exist at all. Most spend their lives in pain and sickness. They literally gasp for air from the day they are born to the day they die. Their average life-span is less than 40 years, while the average Domecilian lives to 97 years of age.

Considering the number of new Domes constructed on our planet over the past few years and the continued success of our zero population growth program, we are now capable of bringing hundreds of thousands of Outsiders into our Domecile system. Life under a Dome for them would mean health and happiness. It would offer them hope and dignity. Entrance into Domecile would not only benefit them, but it would benefit us. Let us not forget that many of the marvelous technological inventions we use today were originally developed by them. Even the Dome itself was invented by one of them in the twentieth century—a man named Buckminster Fuller. I'm convinced that given half a chance they could contribute much to our way of life.

The question of whether or not to allow the Outsiders in is being debated throughout Domecile. We have made great advances technologically, but as social beings I'm afraid things haven't progressed much in our world. Bigoted Domecilians refer to the Outsiders as "Smogites," and make jokes about their gray-white coloring. They argue that, in addition to their strange look, Outsiders have a distinctly "white" odor that is offensive to Domecilians. People complain, too, of their bad personal habits, such as public coughing and spitting.

Now let us take an objective look at our prejudices. Their gray-white coloring is due simply to the fact that, in addition to their being of poor health generally, the atmosphere is so polluted that very little sunlight filters through to give them coloring. As a boy I was acquainted with a number of Outsiders through an aunt, who before the Great War was employed as a servant by an Outsider. In those days before the Domes were necessary, their skin color ranged from a dark tan to a rather pleasing shade of pink. I'm convinced, too, that their personal habits would improve after a reasonable exposure to life inside a Dome where they could develop healthier bodies and lungs.

Another thing to remember is that the few Outsiders who have been admitted into the Dome because of needed skills have adjusted quite well, although it takes a while for them to get used to the oxygen-rich air.

As your pastor, I would like you to consider the Outsider question in the light of the Christian faith. In his letter to the Ephesians, Paul wrote: "For he is our peace, who has made us both one, and has broken down the dividing wall of hostility."

As long as we keep the Outsiders out of our Domes, life for us will be less than it should be. As long as we continue to separate ourselves from the Outsiders we will always live in fear of them, and we will have no peace. Furthermore, when we lock needy men out of our Dome we discover that we are also locking out God. In spite of our riches and improved environment, when we deny the brotherhood of man, we also deny the Fatherhood of God; and life becomes lonely and empty and meaningless. Surely by now we should have learned the lesson of history. A world of Outsiders and Insiders is a terrible, cold, gloomy, and frightening place.

It was precisely such divisions that brought our world close to total destruction in the Great War. Before the war men were divided into nations, races, religions, social and economic classes. Individual nations were divided north and south, rich and poor, white and colored. In those days men built all kinds of barriers—some visible, most invisible. History mentions a Berlin Wall, Iron and Bamboo Curtains, a Mason-Dixon Line, invisible lines separating North and South Korea, and North and South Vietnam. Invisible walls were built in even small communities to keep certain people and groups out of exclusive organizations, neighborhoods, and even churches.

Now we who live free under the Dome have walled out the Outsiders. Won't we ever learn that Christ came in order to tear down the barriers of separation between men as well as between men and God?

The message of Ephesians is that Christ has broken down the barriers that separate Outsiders and Insiders. Jesus Christ does not bring victory to the man who is either inside or outside the Dome. We Domecilians cannot claim Christ solely for ourselves. In Christ, the Insiders and Outsiders are to be brought together as one people. Christ's victory is for all or for none.

In the apostle Paul's time there was in Jerusalem, between the temple proper and the court of the Gentiles, a stone wall on which this inscription in Greek and Latin was written: "No man of another race is to proceed within the partition and enclosing wall about the sanctuary; and anyone arrested there will have himself to blame for the penalty of death which will be imposed as a consequence."

Now, over two thousand years have passed, and we live inside a Dome whose entrances are guarded with this warning: "No Outsider shall enter this Dome without permission of the Domeciliary upon penalty of death."

As Christians we must share in Christ's task—we must do all we can to open our Domes to all men. To share in Christ's ministry of reconciliation, to break down the barriers, is not always easy and is always risky. Yet Christ has called us to this mission and breathed into us the spiritual breath that will give us the strength to carry on.

In closing, let me share with you a very personal experience. Early in my ministry I responded to the church's call to witness to the Outsiders. They welcomed me into their village and shared what little they had with me. Their lungs were highly developed, and they could sustain life without special equipment. For me, an oxygen mask was essential at all times. I awakened one morning in a fright, gasping for air. My breathing apparatus had become defective due to long exposure to pollutants. Seeing my plight, a young Outsider placed his lips over mine and breathed into my mouth. He continued this procedure until they were able to return me to the Dome and safety. I was grief-stricken to learn a few weeks later that his gift of breath to me had so weakened him that he became ill and died of a lung condition.

This young man gave his life for me just as Christ gave his life for all of us. As we share the bread, the wine, and the breath of the Spirit, let us be reminded that the Outsiders in our world need these things, too, in addition to needing bread, water, and breath to sustain them physically.

Let us do all we can to open the Dome to the Outsiders, so that one day all men can live in peace and mutual trust to share the God life and the good life.

•

A Freedom Sermon

The chancel setting is simple: an altar table adorned by a cross and flanked by three chairs. Celebrants 1, 2, and 3, seated in the chairs, are attired in black robes. Number 1 is a woman. She rises, walks to the table, intones, "The Lord is in his holy temple. Let all the earth keep silence before him." *She returns to her seat, and number 2 walks to the center and bids the congregation sing a hymn,* "We Gather Together," *the last stanza of which is:*

> We all do extol thee, thou leader triumphant,
> And pray that thou still our defender wilt be.
> Let thy congregation escape tribulation;
> Thy name be ever praised! O Lord, make us free!

(The third figure rises, walks to center, and solemnly announces—)

3: Let us pray. Merciful Father in heaven, we come before you today—

2: Free!?! *(softly, with scoffing)*

The Rev. Ms. Ann Denham, a United Methodist minister active in the women's liberation movement, resides at 919 Occidental Drive, Claremont, California 91711.

3: —to ask your blessing.

2: Free!?! (*a chuckle; claps hand over mouth*)

3: (*Pause*) We know you are always more ready to hear our prayers than we are to pray, and we—

2: Free! O Lord—free! (*He slides down in his chair and breaks out laughing.*)

(*The woman, seated, leans past the altar table and hisses—*)

1: Don't break down now. We've a long way to go.

(*Figure 2 makes some effort at restraint. Number 3 continues*)

3: We are grateful. We know we have not deserved your love. And we give you our thanks. Our Father, we ask your blessing upon our fellowship and upon every family represented here. Bless those who—

2: Here comes the pitch. Not even God is free.

3: (*stops his praying and turns to 2*) Just what do you think you're doing? Try to hold up your end of things. Do you want them to suspect?

2: Suspect?! They haven't noticed a thing.

(*He folds his arms, stretches out his legs and slouches down in his chair. His legs are bare and hairy. He wears sneakers and no socks. Number 1 rises, leans forward and peers at the congregation, pointing.*)

1: He's right. Look at them. I move we go home. I'm tired of playing church.

3: But to give up? To just walk out?

2: It is finished.

3: But the service was just beginning.

2: It is finished.

3: (*looks around him, pauses, shrugs*) I don't know how it happened, but you're right.

1: It's phony. We've known it all along.

3: (*nodding slowly*) It has no meaning.

1: Perhaps if we shift things around (*she begins tugging the altar table to one side, toward the front*) and got rid of this thing (*removes the cross and dusts the table with the sleeve of her robe*) . . . . There. Isn't that better? (*Sets the cross on the floor to one side.*)

2: (*nods in agreement*) And we could get rid of these.
   (*He flaps the front of his robe and, rising from the chair, begins to take it off. Underneath he is wearing raggedy shorts, a faded T-shirt, and sneakers with no socks.*)

1: Be who we are! (*She takes off her robe, revealing a bright, peasant-style mini-dress. She kicks off her shoes.*)

2: Express ourselves!

3: Tell it like it is! (*He too removes his robe. He is wearing slacks, sport shirt, shoes, and socks.*) We're free! (*Forced and a little strained. He collects the robes and places them to one side.*)

(*They all stand awkwardly, in silence, for a moment.*)

1: If only we had a rock band.

2: Or a guitar.

3: We *said* we want to be who we are.

1: But we still need forms. A language.

3: And something to say.

2: (*returns to his seat and slouches down in his chair*) For worship you need a God, and ours is dead.

3: Not dead—in bondage. Religion is a scheme for controlling him. Manipulating his favor. Usurping his power.

2: Nobody believes that any more. Magic is through.

1: You wanted to set him free! (*points a finger at 2*)

2: (*jumping up*) I wanted to *be* free. Me, free (*thumping his chest*).

3: But you said "God, free."

2: For crying out loud, a figure of speech!

1: Well. How shall we do it?

(*They look around and at each other.*)

3: We haven't much left but words.

2: Talk is cheap.

1: We could be silent.

(*There is a long, awkward pause.*)

2: OK. Here's what we do. We'll write the formulations that religion uses to work God on slips of paper. Then we'll burn them, setting God free.

3: Symbolically, of course.

2: Look. If you have a better idea—

1: We have to do something. They (*points at congregation*) won't leave until they hear a benediction.

3: It's different.

1: It's in!

3: It's very in (*quietly, evenly*).

Number 3 begins tearing slips of paper. Number 1 begins writing. Number 2 scouts the front of the room and returns with a large brass bowl. He places it on the table and centers it. After some hesitation, he drags the altar table to the center front of the room. The slips are placed in the bowl. Number 2 produces matches from his pocket and the three gather around the table. He strikes a match and holds it as it continues to burn, blowing it out at the last second.)

1: (*with awe*) The magic is very strong.

2: Well (*shrugs*). It seems we should at least read them.

3: We think we don't believe. (*Walks away from the altar.*) But we continue to believe (*turning back*)

45

in our own power, our power to manipulate God.

2: That's not true.

3: Oh, isn't it? What were you thinking? Why did you hesitate?

1: (*volunteering*) What if it's true?

3: (*agreeing*) What if it works?

2: (*fearfully and almost inaudibly*) What if we offend?

1: (*turning aside, chanting softly*)

> what if the dawn of the doom of a dream
> bites this universe in two
> peels forever out of his grave
> and sprinkles nowhere with me and you?

2: What if he is truly bound to his word?

3: The word we know.

2: Shall we then set him free?

1: (*turning back*) The power of the name. To know it is to possess the power.

3: The secret name, which exalts the few above the the many.

2: But isn't this his gift? The name, given to certain men? Ask in my name!

1: (*slowly, feeling her way*) The name points beyond itself to the gift. The gift is freedom.

2: (*some understanding dawning*) Even from the name.

3: God allows no one to come making claims. Only by giving up his claim can man stand free.

(*At this point the congregation, if it is to participate, writes personal formulations about God, which are then collected and placed in the bowl. The three figures regroup at the altar table and pick up some of the slips of paper. As the papers are read, they are replaced in the bowl.*)

3: "God is the word which gathers into presence, unifying the modes of time."

2: "God is the Holy Trinity, three persons of one substance."

1: "God is the Father of our Lord and Savior, Jesus Christ."

2: "Our Father."

1: (*softly*) "Abba."

2: (*quietly, as if surprised*) I'm afraid.

1: Take my hand. (*He does.*)

(*Number 2 finally strikes a match and ignites the slips of paper.*)

2: This rough magic I abjure.

3: All our charms are now o'erthrown.

Music begins softly, then with more volume as the fire burns out. It is the Fifth Dimension rock version of "People Got to Be Free." Tentatively the three figures begin to move to the beat. They begin to dance. The solemn twirling dance of sacred dancers gradually gives way to a free style. (The congregation, if participating, may be encouraged to join them.) A second record is introduced, with the song blended into the first so that it slowly merges. This is the Malcolm Dodd Singers in a swinging version of "He's Got the Whole World in His Hands." It builds to a frenzied conclusion, leaving the dancers spent and free, with arms stretched upward and heads thrown back.

Quietly, the whole group joins hands in a circle. Number 1 intones, as benediction, the lines from e.e. cummings:

> —all nothing's only our hugest home;
> the most who die, the more we live

Two Advent Homilies

1. *Homily on Luke 1:45-65*

H: Well, there's the lesson. What a beautiful thing it is!

S: Beautiful!

H & S: Beautiful!

(Pause)

S: What do you think we should do with it?

H: Suppose we got everybody here to say together, "Beautiful!"

S: Not enough.

H: Why not?

S: We weren't asked to be cheerleaders.

H: I know preachers who aren't even that.

S: We weren't asked to be sociologists, either.

H: Should we try a little biblical scholarship, then?

S: Such as?

H: Well, the *Magnificat* was undoubtedly a hymn of the early church. We don't know who wrote it, but we can be very sure that the original Mary wouldn't have been up to such magnificent rhetoric.

S: Depends on how well she knew her Hebrew scriptures. I'm sure *you* have compared it with the song of Hannah in I Samuel.

Dr. Julian Hartt is Noah Porter Professor of Philosophical Theology, and Dr. Don E. Saliers is Professor of Practical Theology, at Yale Divinity School, New Haven, Connecticut 06510.

H: You'd better believe it. I thought there might be something there for us, first thing.

S: It may have inspired Mary—

H: —but it hasn't inspired me.

S: What a pity we know so much!

H: This isn't a night for sarcasm.

S: Sorry about that. I mean I'm sorry you thought I was being sarcastic.

H: You weren't?

S: No. I meant just what I said. We have to climb over our scholarship to get at the realities in the text. That's a pity.

H: All right, then.

S & H: Let's swear off—for tonight.

(*Pause*)

H: What strikes you as real in the text?

S: I was afraid you'd never ask. Well, first, the wonderful amount of *welcoming* going on in the whole business.

H: You know, I never thought of it—

S: —probably because it is so obvious—

H: —but there *is* an unbelievable amount of welcoming here. Even when people are scared by the guest. You know, angels must have been pretty intimidating—

S: —until they were demythologized—

H: —but nonetheless they were *welcomed*.

S: Why not? They were loaded with good news. The greatest, in fact. Wouldn't *you* welcome even an intimidating undemythologized angel loaded with the greatest news?

H: Now who is playing fast—and loose—with the story? Even an angel has to be made welcome before he can unpack.

S: You know, I never thought of that—

49

H: —probably because it is so obvious—

S: —but *of course* that's the way of it! Welcome first, then the news.

H: Come to think of it, lots of people are welcomed, as well as those formidable presences, the angels.

S: Indeed. Nobody wanders around looking for a welcome without getting one. Angels visit shepherds. Welcome! Shepherds visit proud parents. Welcome! The Holy Spirit visits Mary. Welcome! Cousins meet. Welcome! Even little John-in-the-womb does his best to welcome mother-to-be Mary.

H: Wow! Welcome everywhere! Welcome everybody!

(*Pause*)

S: Not quite.

H: There's a shadow, even so.

S: Yes.

H: Yes.

S & H: No welcome at the inn.

S: Somebody goofed in the reservation department.

H: He should have been fired.

S: Maybe somebody was waiting to be impressed before he made welcome.

H: Then, too?

S: Maybe the inn was booked solid by a convention.

H: I see it now: the Five Hundredth Annual Convention of the Committee for the Welcome for the Messiah will meet at the inn in Bethlehem, December 24 following—

S: That's pretty feeble. Crude, too.

H: No harm intended. That's behind the failure of welcome at the inn.

S: But the sheep and the cattle and the donkeys all were kind. In the stable the welcome was warm.

H: That's not scriptural. Anyway, you confuse welcome with animal heat.

S: Not so. It's a matter of making a start. In the bleak midwinter animal heat is a good start.

H: I got it. You want the whole show in on the welcoming.

S: Why not? That's what Mary is all about.

H: So you're not worried by the closed-door policy of the inn?

S: No. Anyway, preachers have worked it to death. "Oh my, oh my, no room in the inn. No room in the inn for the son of God!" For whom do they want us to weep, anyway?

H: Good point. Wherever Christ is born, *that* is the throne of God!

S: Wait a minute! What I meant was, the people of Christ —animals, too—can improvise endlessly to make a place for him. First Mary and Joseph amidst the friendly, warm, curious animals. Thereafter, the world.

H: Now *you* wait a minute! There's another shadow, friend. By name, Herod.

S: Oh, we'll get to him. Or he to us. But now, and first, make sure of the welcome.

H: Oh, yes. Thank God he did.

S: Thank God.

H: For what?

S: For coming to welcome all and sundry.

H: I'll buy that.

S: You can't. It's free.

S & H: Thank God!

2. *Homily on Matthew 2:1-23*

S: A shadow moves in the birthing night.

H: Full of violence, full of fright.

51

S: O obscene darkness,

H: Monstrous, vile,

S: What do you fear

H: From the holy child?

(Pause)

S: Once in a Christmas pageant I played Herod's part so enthusiastically the congregation hissed.

H: Loathsome creature!

S: Once the Adult Bible Class got very upset when I said that as a historical figure Herod wasn't *all* bad.

H: Fiendish butcher!

S: Well, yes. But that business of the slaughter of the innocents was made up. Even in the Scriptures only Matthew tells it.

H: Once is enough. One wonders that so artful a beast as Herod didn't suppress the story altogether. It shows that the truth will come out.

S: Mostly it shows that Herod gets under *your* skin. That's rather odd, you know.

H: No more so than your putting in a good word for him. I would have hissed, too.

S: Wait a minute! I am merely saying it strikes me as odd that Herod still upsets you.

H: Sounds as if you think I am not sufficiently mature or historically objective or scholarly or something.

S: No, no, *no!* Please credit me with enough sense for the proprieties not to go into such things *here*. All I am saying is: you *know* how the story comes out. Herod's wicked cunning scheme fails. And its failing is no accident. Perhaps if he had known the magnitude of his enemy he would have asked the wise man to lead a seminar on unidentified moving stars, and then taken an Excedrin and simply *dreamed* his evil.

H: Implausible. Herod's kind act out their dreams—and leave their hellish stink in public places. His kind pollutes the air of history. The smell of his corruption still emanates from the pages of the Scriptures.

S: Now at last the issue is out in the open. We never were arguing over the historical credibility of Herod.

H: Right.

S: The question is, Whose is the Game?

H: The question is, To whom does the story belong? Tell me truly, would *you* have written in a part for Herod?

(Pause)

H: I think I can guess why you played the part so convincingly.

S: No, you can't. Anyway, the part plays itself. It's a natural. Try it sometime, If you haven't already—

H: That sounds *ad hominem.*

S: I meant it to be personal.

H: The point?

S: Not you alone. All of us. Use your word: history. Herod's kind, as you put it, can't be written off. Of course they're monsters, big or little. But they *are* human. Therefore Herod belongs in the story of Jesus Christ.

H: If he had not existed it would have been necessary to invent him.

S: Herod, you mean. Yes. But the story absorbs him, it does not invent him. There was a Herod—several, in fact. They are best remembered—hisses, oddly passionate hatred, and all—because they are taken up into Christ's story.

H: You mean they are remembered so by us, here, people of the faith, more or less.

S: Yes, oh, *yes.*

53

H: Doesn't it seem odd, though, to go to such pains to remember the vile, the monstrous? No? No. The story is
told, all of it, for all of us.

S: We are all in it—

H: It is for us, every one—

S: But it belongs to Christ.

H: People like us, more or less—

S: —more gullible, no doubt—

H: —told it, and tell it. But he *lived* it. And lives it.

S: Yes. In us. Through us. For us, still.

H: Any chance for Herod?

S: To win? No. The best he can do is arouse our fears.

H: He won't catch Baby Jesus. As you say, the story is tilted
against him.

S: He can't catch Baby Jesus. But he can catch us, in the
net of fear.

H: And make us doubt that he and we are now, and forever, in Christ's story. Well, by God! he shan't catch us
tonight!

S: So say we all: Swear it. Vow it. Pray it.

(*Pause*)

H: A shadow moves in this birthing night.

S: Full of violence, full of fright.

H: But lo! in that cradle.

S: Forgathers God's might.

H: Breaks out God's light.

S: This was the scene when the King was born.

H: Herod stirs in his haunted sleep—

S: —and crushes innocent lovely life.

H & S: O Blessed Christ! for their sake let us sleep in peace.
O Blessed Christ! for their sake let us walk in light.

In God's Hip Pocket

Luke 1:26-56

Mary was a nice young kid
  a teen-ager, I guess
    who was hanging around the house
      doing her chores
      taking care of the younger kids
nothing special about her . . . at least, nothing special
  until one day she got the word . . .
      the word that she was pregnant.

It took some convincing
  . . . because she knew better
    and
  . . . because she didn't *want* to be pregnant.
    In those days, it meant you were *really* in trouble
    —folks would kick you out of town
    —maybe stone you to death.

The Rev. Roger W. Floyd is Executive Director of the Council of Churches of Greater Bridgeport, Bridgeport, Connecticut 06604.

But . . . she got the word!

> For some wild reason, God had chosen *her* to be
> the mother of his Son.

I don't think Mary was overjoyed with this deal . . .
> at least not in the beginning.

I'm sure there were doubts:

> "Have I gone out of my mind? Is this really happen-
> ing?"
>
> "Was I drugged one night and somebody jumped me?"
>
> "If it's true, what right does God have to do this
> to me without even asking?"

A mixture of anger
> and frustration
> and doubt.

A mixture that built up until Mary just had to talk to
someone.

> So she took off to see her cousin Elizabeth.
>
> > That clinched it!
> >
> > > Elizabeth was bubbling over
> > > with the greatness of what was happening.
> > > GOD WAS REALLY OPERATING . . .
> > > AND *THEY* WERE RIGHT IN THE
> > > MIDDLE OF IT.

Mary was overwhelmed:

> "Hey . . . what about this God of ours!
> > My head is spinning . . .
> > my body aches . . .
> > > at the thought that he
> > > should be this close to me.

56

What about this God of ours!
  He's really something!

You love him . . . and he's on your side . . . he always
  has been.
Here I am, a nothing, but I'm the kind he really goes
  for.
The fat cats . . . he brushes them aside.
The power guys . . . they don't make it with him.
The rich . . . they dribble through his fingers.

But, the little guy
  the poor
  the hungry . . . right there . . . in his hip pocket.

God is rolling . . . just like he said he would be.
God is moving . . . and things are happening."

Mary was convinced that God was rolling . . .
      that God was really doing something . . .
        and she was right!

Mary was convinced that God's use of her
  meant that his focus was on the little guy
          the hungry
          the poor
          the nobody

    and she was right!

God is, and always has been, A REVOLUTIONARY!
God is, and always has been, deeply
        primarily concerned
        with the guy on the bottom.
God is A REVOLUTIONARY . . .
  an instigator . . .
  an agitator.

He wants things to be different for the guy on the bottom.

He wants the hungry to be fed.

He wants the poor to live . . . abundantly . . . as human beings.

He wants the nobody to be lifted up . . . with pride and dignity.

HOW DOES THIS HAPPEN IN OUR DAY AND
AGE?

It would be nice to say that the Christian church wants these things.

It would be nice to say that Christians are
 gathering
 mobilizing
to make these things happen.
It would be nice to say that
 because God wants the hungry to be fed
  then we, as the PEOPLE OF GOD,
  will see that they are fed.

It would be nice . . . but it's not very likely.
100,000 people in our world die of starvation *every day*.
 It is as though . . . *every day* . . .
  the total population of Waterbury, Connecticut
  lay down
  curled up
  clutching their bellies in agony.
Why don't we feed them?
 Well . . . after all . . . it's better to keep our
  surplus grain in the warehouses.
  If you give this food away all over the world,
   you foul up the prices.

Anyhow, who's going to pay? It costs money
    to ship grain to India or South America.
Also, some of those starving people are THE ENEMY.
    You don't feed the enemy . . .
        you let them starve.
    Then they won't be around to fight you.

Hundreds of people, mostly children, are starving in our
    country. Say, in the state of Mississippi.

How can this happen here?
    Well . . . the state of Mississippi decided that these
        were the wrong kind of people, so it
        didn't matter whether they lived or died.
    And . . . the federal government paid $127,000 to a
        Mississippi senator for NOT using his
        land to raise food.

Or, a woman in Waterbury describes it this way:
    "Let me explain about housekeeping with no money.
    For breakfast I give my kids cornflakes with powdered
    milk—or maybe cornbread. The rest of the time we
    eat beans or potatoes or bread. Cabbage or onions
    when they're cheap. My kids aren't starving, but they
    do suffer from malnutrition. And because of that,
    they're going to be sick the rest of their lives."

How can this happen . . . in our state . . . in Waterbury?
    Well, the "fat cats" like you and me
        get richer and richer
        and fight furiously against the taxes
            that would feed the hungry.

That's the way it is . . . in India . . .
        in Mississippi . . .

in Waterbury. . . .
LET THEM STARVE!!!

Where is God in all this?
If what the Bible says is true . . .
and I believe it is . . .
then God is right there *with* the hungry.
One of these days,
the hungry are going to get fed up,
and, with God's blessing,
they will rise up and snatch the food
right out of our fat lips.
It could be different . . . but . . .
since God wants the hungry to be fed
and
since the people of God don't care . . .
it looks like REVOLUTION is the only way.

God wants the hungry to be fed. . . .
God wants the lowly lifted up with pride and dignity.
HOW CAN THIS HAPPEN IN OUR DAY?

It would be nice to say that the Christian church wants
it to happen.
It would be nice to say that because God wants the lowly lifted up . . .
then *we*, as the people of God,
would insist that injustice and discrimination stop.
It would be nice . . . but it's not very likely.

Across the country, the ghettos are getting bigger and
blacker . . .
ghetto schools are getting worse
ghetto housing is literally falling apart
unemployment is two and a half times higher for

Negroes than for whites
white prejudice in our northern communities has always
been there, but now it spews forth . . .
   public
   malicious
   bitter.
Why is this happening in our Christian country?

The black man has an answer.
   Listen, and see if you think it's true.
      "When you white Christians talk to us, we hear you.
      You say 'OUR people and YOUR people
            OUR churches and YOUR churches
            OUR community and YOUR community
            OUR schools and YOUR schools.'
      Then you whites go on to sweetly say:
         'Of course, some of your most spiritual people
            may come to our churches
               (as long as they don't jump up and down)
            and a few of your wealthiest and cleanest people
               can move into our neighborhoods
            (as long as it's very few)
            and a few of your brightest children
               can come to our schools
            (but only when the government insists).'
      And then, we blacks hear you say:
         'Remember, black man . . .
               if we let you in, you'd better say *thank you*
                  and you'd better say it loud
                  and you'd better say it often . . .
               because these are OUR neighborhoods
                  and OUR schools

61

and OUR churches
and don't you ever forget it.
Of course, we all love the same Christ.' "

All this is true of Waterbury, of course.
But let me share with you a more personal experience.

A year and a half ago, I married a young Negro couple.
The two of them together were making about $160
per week,
so they were looking for a fairly nice apartment.

They answered ads by phone.
Landlords at the other end,
detecting a slight southern accent,
slammed down the receiver
cursed at them
shouted filth into their ears.
So, I handled the phone . . .
and made appointments for them to go and see
apartments.
Again and again,
We'd ring the doorbell
the curtains would wiggle
but no one would answer the door.

Or, if they answered the door,
"Sorry, the apartment's taken."
"But, we had an appointment!"
"Someone came after you called."

After five incidents like this, I began to say:
"You say the apartment's taken. Did they put
down a deposit?"
"Yes."

"I don't believe you. I'd like to see the stub,
   if you don't mind."
"I *do* mind!"
"I'd like to see that stub, or I'll call
   the police."
"You do anything you like. But there aren't any
   filthy niggers in this neighborhood ...
      and there aren't going to be.
Now, you get off my porch or I'll boot all three
   of you down the stairs."

Fourteen times in a year and a half this couple
went
      through this degradation.
How much more of this is the black man going to
take?
Where is God in all of this?

If what the Bible says is true ...
   and I believe it is ...
then God is right there on that porch ...
   and in the crumbling alleys
      where these families are forced to live.

God is in the midst of the degraded.
   One of these days
      black people are not going to take this any more,
         and, with God's blessing,
         they will rise up and SMASH the people
            who have oppressed them for centuries.

It could be different.
It doesn't have to happen that way ... but ...
   since God wants the lowly to be lifted up
      and

63

since the people of God can't be bothered . . .
it looks like REVOLUTION is the only way.

I'm sure this is disturbing.
It disturbs me to hear myself say it.
But I believe it's true . . . and it must be said.

We are on the edge of at least two revolutions:
the poor against the rich
the black against the white.

That puts *us* on the receiving end of both.

ARE THESE REVOLUTIONS NECESSARY?

Maybe not!

If Christians across the world don't turn their backs
on the poor and hungry . . .
there is hope
and there may still be time.

If we made tractors instead of helicopters
fertilizer instead of napalm . . .
If we shipped wheat instead of bullets . . .
If we sent farmers and teachers instead of soldiers . . .
the food would be there
and the poor wouldn't have to fight
for something to eat.

But I'm afraid it's not going to happen.
There are too many companies getting rich on
bombs.
There are too many generals who wouldn't have anything to do
if there wasn't someone to kill.
There are too many who want the wars

and too few who care about the nameless
    millions who are starving.

So, inevitably, the hungry will rise up
    and demand their share.

    Would you expect them to do anything else?
Would you expect them to whimper and slink away
    watching their children starve to death
      before their very eyes?

No! One of these days
    they'll look around to find out
      who's got the food . . .
      who's keeping it from them . . .
    then they'll come after us . . .
      us . . . you and me!

And the blacks . . .
    that didn't have to happen either.
We've been talking brotherhood and equality for
    years.
    If we Christians had taken it seriously
      we could have changed the American scene
      and the black man wouldn't have to FIGHT
        for his place in our society today.

But we didn't!
    And because we didn't . . .
      the voices in the ghetto are shouting
      REVOLUTION.

Are these revolutions necessary?
    Yes . . . because we, in our selfishness . . .
      in our arrogance . . .
        have made them necessary.

ARE THESE REVOLUTIONS EVIL? ARE THEY WRONG?

Because we are on the receiving end,
    it's pretty easy to believe that they are wrong.

But our biblical faith says . . . NO!
    These revolutions are the work of God . . .

        God's judgment upon us . . .
        God's concern for the poor and lowly.

Remember what Mary said . . .
    setting the stage for the coming of Christ:

        God stretched out his mighty arm
            and scattered the proud people with all their
                plans,

        He brought down mighty kings from their thrones,
            and lifted up the lowly.

        He filled the hungry with good things
            and sent the rich away with empty hands.

        This is the way God operates . . .

        WHERE DOES IT LEAVE US?

A Zero Died

Sally Martin is dead!
Do you hear me?
Sally Martin is dead.
But there I go.
How should I expect you to know,
  or for that matter to care.
You never knew Sally.

I read about her death in an out-of-town newspaper.
There was no picture.
The story didn't rate the front page.
In fact, I almost missed it completely.
But there it was: 13 lines in all
        over in the back section
        among the recipes and "For Sale" items
        near the "Help Wanted" ads.
    Sally Martin is dead . . .
    a local resident . . .
    after a brief illness . . .

The Rev. George K. Jones is minister of Arlington United Methodist Church, Nashville, Tennessee 37217.

in the County Hospital . . .
two brothers and one niece survive . . .
funeral conducted by the Rev. such-and-such . . .
such-and-such funeral home in charge of the arrangements.
There it was—the bare facts
13 lines among the recipes and "For Sale" items
near the "Help Wanted" section
13 lines in the back section
13 lines with 5 words per line
64 words in all: her name
then why her name was listed (because she's dead)
then where she died
where she lived
the 3 survivors
then the name of the minister and the funeral
home.
13 lines,
32 spaces per line
64 words over near the "Help Wanted" ads.
Not much recognition for 55 years,
just over a word a year . . .
near the "Help Wanted" ads.
Good Lord! Near the "Help Wanted" ads!

Now I haven't heard from anyone who attended the
funeral.
You can't tell much from 64 words that cover 55 years
plus the funeral.
64 words.
The same paper carried the story of a wedding.
It took 213 words just to describe the bride's gown.

In the news section, 305 words were given to the new
    water tank in a neighboring town.
There were 252 words telling about a new store.
Cabbage at 5¢ a pound received twice the space of
    Sally's obituary.
A fertilizer ad got ten times the space.
Later, the ad for the disposal of her home
    received 21 times the space given to the disposal
    of the owner of the home.

In my mind's eye, though, I didn't need any more words.
I could picture it as though I were there.
Her bleeding ulcer acted up again.
She either couldn't, or didn't,
    go to the doctor until it was too late.
The doctor tried to be good to Sally.
He never sent her a bill.
But you know how that goes—
    because she wasn't paying,
    she failed to go as often as she needed.
By the time she went,
    her hemorrhage was probably too far along.
Ulcers . . .
Ulcers from all her worries.
When her mother died the brothers wanted to sell the
    house,
    with its three apartments,
    and divide the estate.
But selling the family home didn't strike Sally just
    right
      so she took her meager savings
      and sold her car

and mortgaged away the rest of her life
to buy the homeplace.
She was a sitter by trade.
She sat up with sick people at night.
She sold greeting cards and gifts on the side.
And all went well—for awhile.

But you know how old houses are.
Major repairs soon came along and her money was gone.
There wasn't enough for mortgage
     and repairs
     and normal living,
      so normal living had to go.
She cut a meal each day
   and used hardly any heat at all.
When the radio and TV quit,
  they weren't repaired.
Then a tenant moved,
   and since there was no money to redecorate,
   the apartment remained empty,
   and now there was still less income.

The old family home, and only Sally cared.
And we say it's crazy,
  but how can we understand?
We think that this sacrifice for a house is rather sense-
less.
  But then, of course, we're fortunate enough to have
      a mother or father,
      or son or daughter,
      or husband or wife,
      or brother or sister who cares.
The old homeplace, this was Sally's family,

and, as the ceremony says,
"until death us do part."

And her sitting fell off too.
As she worried, she became sick,
    and how can a sick sitter help the sick?
And some said that her sitting fell off
    because she had become a grouch,
    and that people quit coming to see her
            or speaking much
    because they would be grouched at.
Oh, how shallow is our perception!!
Her grouchiness was only a cover.
She didn't want people coming
        when she had no heat
        and with the wallpaper hanging from the ceiling.
And then look at her patients!
As the demand for her services fell,
    she could get only the problem cases,
    only those who chased off about two sitters a week,
    only those who acted like the devil incarnate.
She had to take them,
        with their grumpy dispositions
        and spoiled natures
        and bad manners
        and all.
She was forced to swallow her pride.
She needed the work.
On one occasion, she worked 136 straight days for
    one such ill-humored man.
    She walked in the rain and in the snow.
    She had to.
    She needed the job.

Every day of it.
There could be no time for rest.
Yes, she needed the money,
    but there was also something within her that made
    her faithful
        even to an old reprobate.
You see, they were sharing the same lonely,
        agonizing path.

You say that she was a grouch. . . .
Well, her bark had no bite,
    and her frown was only skin deep.
Underneath was a person
        and a personality
        and a sense of humor.
  I remember her Christmas card from three years back.
    There it was, imprinted so boldly, "Sally and Ar-
    thur,"
    and I thought to myself,
    "That sly fox has got married."
    But then it struck me,
    she was giving recognition to her other lifelong com-
    panion—
    Arthritis.

Now about the funeral.
I'm sure that it was in the small side parlor at the funeral
  home.
The brothers from out of state weren't there.
They asked the niece to make the arrangements.
After all, they hadn't been there in ten years
    and wouldn't know much about it.
    And besides,
    they needed to save their trip

for the settling of the estate.
The undertaker was asked to choose the pallbearers.
 He knew who could take off work to come.
 She was so frail.
 Six would be more than enough.
There were some flowers.
 There was one spray from the church down the street,
  which had a big white streamer
 with the name of the church in gold letters.
 The niece commented on their thoughtfulness
  and how they must have thought well of Sally.
 The undertaker didn't tell her
  that they always sent a spray
  with a white streamer
  with the name of the church in big gold letters
  no matter who it was.
 How kind.
 They never failed in their ministry.
 To qualify, all one had to do was die—
  then the flowers
  with a big white streamer
  with the name of the church in gold letters.
But really, there weren't many flowers.
 Many of the patients for whom she had cared
  had never received flowers from Sally.
 Most of the rest were selfish
  who never gave anybody anything
  but a hard time.
 And her acquaintances . . .
  had slowly dwindled away.
  And after all,
   why should Sally have expected many flowers?
   She was a grouch.

A few flowers,
a niece,
the minister,
six pallbearers,
Sally,
and a handful of acquaintances,
  all together in the small side parlor at the funeral
   home
  with room to spare.
"And Parson," commented the niece,
 "please make it brief.
 No long eulogy.
 I like a short funeral.
 They're so much more appropriate,
  and besides,
  I've got to head on back home."

But the minister knew Sally, and for Sally he said,
" 'Lord, when did we see thee hungry and feed thee,
 or thirsty and give thee drink?
 And when did we see thee a stranger and welcome
  thee?
 And when did we see thee sick
  or in prison
  and visit thee?
Inasmuch as ye did it unto the least of these. . . .'
'Come, O blessed of my Father, and inherit the kingdom
 prepared for you from the foundation of the world.' "
And the minister also said,
" 'But Lord, when did we fail to minister unto thee?
. . . Truly I say unto you,
  as you did it not unto the least of these,
  you did it not to me.

Depart from me, you cursed, into the eternal fire
   prepared for the devil and his angels.' "
And then the procession . . .
and the dirt . . .
and then 13 lines
    with 64 words
    among the recipes
    and "For Sale" items
    near the "Help Wanted" section.

Well, I guess there's really small reason for you to be
   interested.
   You didn't know *this* Sally,
   but I did.
And, as I was reading the obituary,
   there was a note on the kitchen counter,
   a reminder from my wife,
   it had been there for three weeks.
   "Write Sally and thank her for the Christmas gift."
Yes, she had sent me some stationery.
It was as though I had part of her estate.
But I hadn't taken time to write the note.
You see, I was busy.
And so there it was,
    13 lines
    with 5 words to a line,
    64 words in all
      over among the recipes
      and the "For Sale" items
   right next to the "Help Wanted" section.

The "Detroit" Parable

This brief sermon was originally part of a much longer multi-media show featuring light, sound, and slides. It consisted of several slides of each of three automobiles, viewed from different angles, with the following text on a tape recording. The first car was an old black sedan, of foreign origin, which had obviously received hard treatment through the years. The second was a small yellow car of Oriental make. The third was a sleek American limousine. A different voice spoke for each car. The first had a Southern drawl. The second was an imitation of an Oriental accent. The third was confident and smoo-o-o-th.

Hey, man, I'm an old black import. I've been around this country for a pretty long time—and, I'll tell ya, man, I've had it pretty rough. Look at my body, all dented, bruised, and beat up. Look at my spare tire, showing signs all over of being driven hard. And not only that, I'm pretty dirty. Can you imagine, my owner put me to work down in the fields of Alabama, and he didn't even clean me up after all that work! Yeah, my history over in this country hasn't really been too great. Maybe it wouldn't have been so bad, but my owner just hasn't treated me right.

The Rev. Lawrence Balleine is a student at Vanderbilt Divinity School, Nashville, Tennessee 37240.

Hi. I'm a pretty recent import to this country. As you can see, I'm pretty small and don't have much power at all. But my owner likes me because he can control me quite easily. I'm also inexpensive to run, so all too often I'm just considered my owner's second car. I'm not really enjoyed for what I am myself, but only as a means of doing the job cheaper. I do wish my owner would give me more credit than that.

Hi. I'm the typical white, Anglo-Saxon, middle-class automobile. Look at how big I am! Look at how bright and shiny I am! And man, have I got power! Look at my smooth lines—not a scratch on them. And not one dent on my entire body. Notice my tires—not at all blistered. I guess my owner has really been good to me. I've really been well taken care of. Yes, I guess I've really got it pretty damn good!

Meet the Distinctive Light

As he went on his way Jesus saw a man blind from his birth. His disciples put the question, "Rabbi, who sinned, this man or his parents? Why was he born blind?" "It is not that this man or his parents sinned," Jesus answered; "he was born blind so that God's power might be displayed in curing him. While daylight lasts we must carry on the work of him who sent me; night comes, when no one can work. While I am in the world I am the light of the world."

With these words he spat on the ground and made a paste with the spittle; he spread it on the man's eyes, and said to him, "Go and wash in the pool of Siloam." (The name means "Sent.") The man went away and washed, and when he returned he could see.

His neighbours and those who were accustomed to see him begging said, "Is not this the man who used to sit and beg?" Others said, "Yes, this is the man." Others again said, "No, but it is someone like him." The man himself said, "I am the man." They asked him, "How were your eyes opened?" He replied, "The man called Jesus made a paste and smeared my eyes with it, and told me to go to Siloam and wash. I went and washed, and gained my sight." "Where is he?" they asked. He answered, "I do not know."—John 9:1-12 NEB

Dr. Wayne Hensley is professor of preaching at Minnesota Bible College, Rochester, Minnesota 55901.

Have you ever thought about how this miracle in the ninth chapter of John might have been reported if the Jews had had television? Hold on to your imaginations and let's see if we can recreate the event and its significance as if we were watching a news special on Jerusalem television.

"Good morning. At this time WJEW-TV brings you a special news report on an unusual event that occurred yesterday here in the capital city. Your host for this special report is capital news correspondent Benjamin Maccabeus—Mr. Maccabeus."

"Thank you, and good morning. Welcome to our special report entitled, 'Meet the Distinctive Light.' Before we proceed with our program, let me introduce to you our guests who compose the panel to discuss the events of yesterday. On my left is Mr. Caleb Nazareth, veteran news analyst from Galilee; on my right is Mr. Moses Arnon, who covers a beat in Trans-Jordan; and to my extreme right is Professor Abraham Reubenstein of the Jerusalem Torah Seminary.

"Yesterday, a blind beggar was reported to have recovered his sight. Rumors have it that Old Manasseh, as he is known to many Jerusalemites, a man who was born blind and has made his living begging in the streets of Jerusalem for many years, was suddenly and miraculously healed. Credit for the miracle has been attributed to Jesus, the Nazarene, who has created quite a stir wherever he has gone.

"Caleb Nazareth, since you work the Galilee scene, could you enlighten us about this fellow Jesus?"

"Yes, Ben, I've attended a few of his crusades and have some impressions. I have heard him say that he is

79

the light of the world. He seems to equate this image with the Shekinah glory which symbolized the presence of Jehovah in the old Tabernacle. If this miracle actually happened, it might well be a vivid demonstration that Jehovah's personal presence and power have come into our lives. As I have reported various events in our nation, I have noticed that one of the greatest defects from which our people suffer is being blind to the realities of life.

"You know, Ben, this Jesus might just be the one to make our people aware of the blindness from which they suffer. So many of them go to the synagogues regularly, though they have no real goal in life. Perhaps they are blind to the reality of Jehovah and aren't aware of it. Life can become pretty petty when we don't see beyond our own religious and social noses. One thing we can say about this Jesus is that he drives us out of our ruts when we come face-to-face with him."

"Thank you, Caleb. Mr. Arnon, would you care to elaborate on this aspect of the Nazarene? Does he really bring a light from Jehovah which reveals spiritual defects in people?"

"Yes, Ben. We know that our prophets of old often acted out parables to drive home their messages. Perhaps the healing of this man's physical blindness was just such an acted-out parable. I interviewed some of the beggar's neighbors yesterday evening. In light of the assumed miracle I was amazed at their indifference. Perhaps the events reveal that they are blinded by indifference. I'm reminded of a statement made by one of my professors when I attended the Perean School of Journalism. He said that an enthusiastic student is heavenly to a teacher, a hostile student is hopeful, but an indifferent student is hopeless. I suppose that the same is true of so many people in all walks of life. So many souls are covered with the cobwebs of contentment that they need someone to show them how blind they really are. Maybe, Ben, this Jesus is just the one to do it."

"Gentlemen, let's pause here and switch to our mobile unit for an on-the-spot interview with Rabbi Zebulun Hyman. Reporter Ephraim Goldberg on camel #7 has the interview. Come in, Ephraim."

"This is Ephraim Goldberg at the Via Dolorosa Synagogue. With me is Zebulun Hyman, senior Rabbi of the synagogue, and Vice President of the National Council of Synagogues of Yahweh. Rabbi Hyman, what is your reaction to the events of yesterday?"

"Mr. Goldberg, I pose one key question: How can a man who is a sinner do such signs? This man broke the Sabbath in two distinct ways. One, he engaged in physical labor by mixing the clay out of dirt and spittle. Two, he attempted to practice medicine, and without a license at that."

"But, Brother Hyman, if Jesus actually helped this man Manasseh, could his actions be construed to be so flagrant a violation of Jehovah's will?"

"Mr. Goldberg, let me remind you that we have a long and holy tradition to guide our relationship to God. We know that God works through the forms and institutions established by our fathers. If we need any guidance on religious matters, we can consult the profound opinions of our most learned scholars in our commentaries and religious journals."

"Thank you, Rev. Hyman. While Rabbi Hyman and his colleagues feel that the miracle was a fabrication and that Jesus is a charlatan, many people are now questioning the validity of a stringent legalism which concentrates on forms, institutions, and minute details of opinion, while ignoring attitudes, personal relationships, and personal needs. This is reporter Ephraim Goldberg with mobile camel #7 at the Via Dolorosa Synagogue returning you to our studio."

"This is your host, Benjamin Maccabeus, back in the studios of WJEW-TV. I want to pose another question for one of our panelists, Professor Abraham Reubenstein. Professor, earlier Mr. Nazareth spoke about this Jesus claiming to be the manifestation of the Shekinah glory of Jehovah and, as such, discovering some of our most serious spiritual defects. Have you had any contact with him, and has your contact with him given you any insights as to what he thinks he can do about our defects?"

"Mr. Maccabeus, I have been preparing an article for publication concerning some of my impressions along these lines. Let me share a few of my thoughts with you and our viewers. If Jesus can drive out the disorder of physical blindness, it is entirely possible that he can drive out the spiritual disorders of life. If the basic defects of life blind us, then the light is essential to drive out the chaos of disorder created by the darkness. We know how essential light is to life. My distinguished colleague, Professor Riggerman, in an article he .published recently, pointed out that without light, flowers, if they grew at all, would be colorless; animate and inanimate objects would fail; and the world would hasten back to the primeval chaos out of which Jehovah brought light and life. I believe that if this Jesus is the living Shekinah of Jehovah, and if as such he can heal the ills of humanity, replacing spiritual darkness with light and life, it would be the most profound revelation of Jehovah since the Exodus."

"Thank you, Professor. In order to look at some of the disorders which plague modern lives we now switch to roving reporter, Mary Esther Asher, on mobile camel #3. Come in Mary Esther."

"This is Mary Esther Asher at the Jerusalem sheep gate, one of the busiest gates in the city. I have interviewed several people, both citizens and travelers, during the last few hours. The interviews disclose that one of the most serious disorders of our society is disillusionment. For many centuries our people have been looking for the fulfillment of the national golden dream. The long-awaited messiah and his earthly utopia have not come. Many of our prominent Sadducees and rabbis are proclaiming that Jehovah is dead. Our nation has experienced war in almost every generation since our return from exile. Government bureaucracy, corruption, and abuse have increased. Frequently, our disillusionment takes the form of riots and rebellions. Earlier this year the S.D.S. (Students for a Decalogue Society) rioted and took over the University of Palestine, and last month the notorious Barabbas led a rebellion of Hebrew Nationalists against the Roman establishment. Sociologists and theologians now tell us that this disillusionment is leading to an increase in suicides, while the producers of tranquilizers, stimulants, and sleeping pills grow rich.

"Another disorder that seems to characterize our society is that of skepticism, with its twin brother escapism. One distinct impression gained from my interviews is that many of our people profess faith in Jehovah, but in their daily practices they divorce piety and practice, separate the sacred and secular, and dig a deep depression

83

between faith and the common life. For many modern men, life is no more than food, drink, and togas; love is sex; happiness is some nebulous peace of mind; and a great vocation is a career in business, sheep herding, politics, or money changing.

"In order to see how this revolutionary teacher Jesus would meet these problems, I have asked one of our prominent rulers, Pharisee Nicodemus, to give his opinion based on his interview with Jesus. Nicodemus, if Jesus is the light of Jehovah, what would he say to us to repair the disorders which threaten to drive us to despair?"

"As you know, Miss Asher, I had a lengthy interview with Jesus one night some time ago. I also have heard him speak on a few other occasions. I think he is saying to our loveless world that the rock-bottom reality of life is love—try it, and see its endurance. To a world gone mad after materialism, he would say that the last word about life is not what you get but what you give."

"Thank you, Mr. Nicodemus. This is Mary Esther Asher at the Jerusalem sheep gate, returning you to our studio and Benjamin Maccabeus."

"Here we are once again in our WJEW studio with the final portion of our special report, 'Meet the Distinctive Light.' We have discussed this remarkable incident which took place yesterday and have attempted to set forth some of the implications of the miracle, if indeed such a miracle actually transpired. It has been suggested that, if Jesus is the revealed light of Jehovah, this miracle may well dramatize that he can discover the defects of life and overcome the disorders caused by the defects. Our final guest is the beggar himself, Manasseh Ben Ezra.

"Manasseh, you certainly have been the center of a

staggering storm since the Sabbath. What is your reaction to all of this?"

"Well, Mr. Maccabeus, of course I am overjoyed to have my sight after a life of blindness, although it saddens me to see the indifference of my neighbors and the hostility of our religious leaders. I do wish that they had not put me out of the synagogue. However, I have found in Jesus something more than my eyesight. Although I only discovered him yesterday, I have already begun to perceive that he is the light of Jehovah who can determine the whole direction of my life. I know that I must now live as a child of the light.

"His disciples have already told me that those who follow him must be lamps through which his light shines to others. I'm not much of a vessel through which his light may shine—a poor, disregarded beggar—but I see that I must use my simple life to tell other blind beggars where to find the light of life. I guess that the only choice any of us has is to bear witness to the light in this world, each one in his own meager place, in his own meager way, with what meager resources and abilities he has. I am determined not to neglect the small segment of the world which is mine.

"Mr. Maccabeus, someone told me that some time ago Jesus said that lights are intended for dark places. I am not going to be like those Essenes who retreated to the wilderness to escape worldly corruption and keep their religion to themselves. I may not make much of a dent in the darkness of this warring, lusting, idolatrous society, but with Jehovah's help, I intend to try."

"Thank you for coming to share your experience with us, Mr. Ben Ezra. Your personal witness to this momentous event has been profoundly stirring.

"And I want to thank our guests, Mr. Caleb Nazareth,

Mr. Moses Arnon, and Professor Abraham Reubenstein. This is your host, Benjamin Maccabeus. Having explored the miracle of yesterday and having looked into its implications, I suppose there is only one question I ought to leave with you. What do *you* think about this mysterious man who claims to be the Distinctive Light?"

A Bridge over Troubled Waters

The setting is the kitchen or dining room table of Pauline Peterson's house. Catherine Chambers calls in the middle afternoon. Over a cup of coffee they sit down for serious conversation.

Scene I

(Pauline takes freshly brewed coffee to table, pours a cup, nibbles a cookie, and reads a magazine while first verse of "Bridge over Troubled Waters" is played. Doorbell rings.)

P: *(Offstage at door)* Catherine! You're just in time for a cup of coffee. I just poured myself a fresh cup.

C: Great. I could use one.

P: Been shopping?

C: No, out to a meeting.

P: Oh.

The Rev. Maurice Fetty is Senior Minister of the Mayflower Congregational Church, Grand Rapids, Michigan 49506.

C: Really a bore too! About 80 percent of all the meetings I go to are such a waste of time—a bunch of gibberish.

P: I'll second that.

C: I don't know when I've ever been so discouraged. I guess that's why I keep going to these meetings— keeps my mind off things, and I keep hoping I'll find some answers at one of them.

P: You have some questions that have been bothering you?

C: Yes—I really have—lots of them . . . . Each evening I look out on the sunset—wondering . . . . There was a time when I thought I had it all sewn up and in the bag—I mean, I thought I knew who I was. Everything seemed to be in its place. My goals were pretty well set and I knew what I had to do to reach them. Now, I'm not so sure. The fact is that underneath it all I'm—well, I'm confused. It's not that I can't see things to do or places to go or people to see. Not at all—I'm pretty well equipped for that. (*Laughs to self.*) Have you ever seen the car of one of those ham-radio operators, or one of their sound studios in their houses? Well, you know they spend thousands of dollars on every conceivable kind of equipment. It's quite a display! The thing I always wonder about when I see all that is—what do they say to each other? I mean, can you imagine a guy from Maine calling out to California, "Hello Joe! This is Henry from Booth Bay Harbor, Maine. How's the weather out there? Snowing here. How's your wife?" and so on. When you think of it, it's just a lot of expensive prattle. Well equipped to speak to anybody, but with nothing to say—really. So you see, I guess that's how I feel. Well equipped with education and money and conveniences, but I don't know what to say. There isn't much that excites me or turns me on any more— I mean, what do you tell your children besides be polite, study hard, and make money?

P: You don't tell your children anything these days. They tell you. But I think I know what you mean. I remember in college psychology they used to call this whole thing an identity crisis. Only in college they used examples from psychiatric wards and adolescents in junior high.

C: And we were always quite sure of our identity.

P: Quite sure. Although I admit I was a bit shaken when I went to college. High school had been a ball. And as a matter of fact I had excelled in a number of things—good grades, good dates, and homecoming queen.

C: And in college? . . .

P: And in college I met a thousand more homecoming queens and at least five hundred who had been on the high school honor roll, not to mention a hundred or so valedictorians and salutatorians.

C: And my high school boyfriend, who was tops in my town, had a hard run to meet the new competition.

P: And mine met his equal several times over. It was a bit of an identity crisis.

C: I guess it was part of coming of age. Something like

89

adolescents leaving childhood for the new world of sexual passion and self-consciousness.

P: Yeah, you like the new experiences. They are both exciting and threatening. I can remember wanting to run up and embrace every male I saw—I had a mad crush on my English teacher. Then I would go home and play with my dolls.

C: That's funny. I can remember—maybe I shouldn't tell you this—but I can remember once in eighth grade, you see, I was pretty well developed by that time, I can remember necking up a storm with a sophomore boy in the park behind the band shell! You know what I did after that? I went home, sat on my Dad's lap, and had him read to me.

P: You wanted both adventure and security!

C: That's it—adventure and security. And I was confident I could get both. There was plenty of adventure with that sophomore boy—whew!—and Dad offered me a lot of security.

P: Well, I guess those are the typical ingredients of an identity crisis—going back and forth between the old and the new, looking for adventure, then running back to the old security when things get too hot. You wonder who you are—a well-endowed lover or Daddy's good little girl. . . .

C: Except it's different now.

P: How do you mean?

C: It's a little hard to define—yes, I guess that's it. It's sort of vague, hard to define. I mean—well—for example, when I was a girl I knew where to find adventure and

I knew where to find security. But now I'm not sure where to find either one. In fact, I'm not sure they're what I want to find.

P: You seem to have security. I mean, from the looks of things, your husband is doing all right.

C: That's true.

P: And in the adventure category—you have a lot of travel, including those two trips to Europe.

C: That's true too. But it's deeper than that now. I'll admit that I'd always hoped for these things. They were a part of those goals I was talking about earlier—goals that were sort of assumed to be right, to be fulfilling.

P: You must surely have found some fulfillment.

C. Fulfillment? Yes, I guess I have. But you know, when we were in Europe—having the trip of our dreams—we were sitting at a sidewalk café in Paris watching people go by, and it came over me, and I said to myself, who am I anyway?

P: I've heard that Paris will do that to you.

C: No, really, maybe it was the presence of history all around us. Here in this country the present moment seems to be the only time thing. But there you sort of find yourself submerged in history, engulfed by it. And you say to yourself, who am I anyway, amongst all these people? All these forgotten people who lived and died before me. Who am I in relation to them?

P: You're Catherine Chambers, happily married to Charlie Chambers, with three healthy little Chamberses.

91

C: Yeah, and you're Pauline Peterson, happily married to Jim Peterson, etc., etc.

(*Doorbell rings*)

P: Oh, there's the doorbell! It always rings at the wrong time. Excuse me, Catherine.

(*At the door in the background.*)

P: Reverend Carter, come in. It's good to see you.

RC: Good to see you too. . . . Oh, I didn't mean to interrupt. I didn't know you had company.

P: Oh, that's all right. I'd like you to meet Catherine Chambers.

RC: Catherine, it's a pleasure to meet you.

P: Catherine and I were just having a chat over a cup of coffee. Can I pour you a cup?

RC: I don't know. I'd heard Jim was still sick and I thought I'd drop by to see how he was doing.

P: Oh, he's doing fine. Went back to work today, in fact. It was nice of you to think of him. . . . Here, have a cup of coffee.

(*An awkward pause.*)

P: Catherine and I were just having an interesting conversation—a bit deep, I might say.

RC: Sounds intriguing.

P: Actually, it was about our—well—

C: Go ahead.

P: —about our identity crisis. It's a matter of concern to both of us. Actually Catherine brought it up. She

92

suggested that (*music gradually up here*) it's something like the identity crisis of adolescence, but not quite.

(*Music up, second verse of "Bridge over Troubled Waters," conversation continues in background.*)

Scene II

C: (*Music down*) So that's about where we were when you came in.

RC: I think you are on to a significant characteristic of our time—we wonder who we are, what our goals should be. We don't seem to have anything to measure ourselves by anymore. I remember my first year of college—I had just about made the adjustment of separation from home when my folks moved from our old homeplace to a new town, a new job, new church, and new friends. I didn't realize the full impact at first, but it eventually caused a kind of trauma in me.

C: A trauma?

RC: Well, yes, to some degree at least. As long as they were in my hometown I had something to measure myself against. I could sort of judge my progress, rest myself on a rather solid and stable past, compare myself against my friends and relatives. When the folks moved, it was as if the whole foundation of my life had been taken out from under me.

P: Think of the poor kids today who have never lived in one place more than three or four years!

RC: Right. What do they measure themselves by? Their peer group keeps changing, new standards are thrown

93

at them all the time—is it any wonder that we have identity crises? Like the writer of Ecclesiastes says, everything is futility, a striving after the wind, be cause everything is change.

C: But, Reverend Carter, I can see your point, and I believe it's a good one. Yet there is something more nagging at me from within. Maybe change is at the bottom of it. With me, I guess it's a loss of a sense of value, of meaning—or purpose. I mean, I don't mind living—at least not most of the time. It's just that nothing consumes me any more. There's nothing that grabs me in an ultimate sense, nothing to which I feel I could really devote myself. . . . I suppose you hear a lot of speeches like that.

RC: Not enough, I'm afraid.

P: Maybe you—we—are looking for the wrong thing. Perhaps there is no absolute person or thing to which we should be devoted. Maybe we should just accept the fact that there are no ultimates in life. Maybe everything is relative and partial, and we should just resign ourselves to the fact.

C: That would be unchristian, wouldn't it, Reverend Carter?

RC: Well, not exactly.

C: Seems to me that's what it's all about. Doesn't Christianity say that it has an Absolute, something definite to which it should be committed? I heard Billy Graham say on TV the other night that a lot of our troubles come from not believing the Bible. And you see lots of church bulletin boards with the caption, "Christ is the Answer."

P: Yeah, my sophomore son came home the other day after seeing one of those and he asked me, "What's the question?"

RC: At least one of the questions is identity.

C: Is Christ the answer to identity? Do you have to believe in him as some sort of ultimate absolute to gain your identity?

RC: Well, yes and no. No, you do not *have* to believe in him. Yes, I believe he helps provide the answer to identity. But I believe we have to be careful about what we mean by the words ultimate and absolute.

P: What do you mean by them?

RC: I mean that when we think of Christ as an absolute, we should not think of him in a static and rigid way. Many people see him as a lawgiver who sets down new laws which must never be broken if we are to be true Christians—should I say, authentic persons. Others see Christ as an absolute, authoritarian teacher who hands down divine lectures, infallible rules which must always be obeyed if we are to be counted among his number.

P: That sounds a lot like the Christ I learned about.

C: So how do you see him, Reverend Carter?

RC: Well, I see Christ more as a dynamic figure than a static one. I don't conceive of him as ordaining any one particular way of life as divine or absolute. Nor do I see him embracing one culture, or class, or political or economic system as ultimate. In that sense I think everything is relative.

95

P: But that seems to leave us hanging in midair.

C: Yes, how do you find your identity if it isn't within a family or culture or a definite, absolute religion?

RC: You find it in the same way Jesus found it—in the pilgrimage of faith. Remember his hottest criticism was addressed to the rigid and static types of his society—the traditionalists and legalists.

P: But our problem today is not rigidity—it's the problem of change.

C: Right. I think women today don't know who they are—wife, mother, career girl, lover, or general chauffeur and household servant. We're confused about our roles.

RC: I agree. Yours is the problem of flux and change. But this very fact can work to your advantage. Hard and frustrating as they are, the fantastic changes of our time have freed you to be a new person, a new breed. In previous times in history this was not even a live option for women. The bondage to the past has been broken in our time. We are free to become something new.

P: But I don't know what to become. I sometimes look wistfully at the security my mother seemed to have. . . . Yet she is critical of me today.

RC: As Jesus' rigid contemporaries were of him. They were judging him, condemning him, from the standpoint of an older order, an old way of seeing things. They were very secure in it. Yet their very security was leading to death. It was old wine in an old wineskin.

C: Then that's why so many religious types are so critical and judgmental today—they have an old, rigid way of seeing things.

RC: Right. Often their judgments are made out of fear. If they lose their systems, their way of life, they will lose their identity.

C: Aha, now I see. That's precisely what has happened to us. Our old systems, our old ways of seeing, are breaking up in the rapid changes and advances of life.

RC: Keep going.

C: Consequently, we are sensing our loss of identity because our identity was tied up with those old systems.

RC: Hear, hear!

P: So how does Jesus fit into all this? Where did he find his identity? Wasn't it in first-century Israel?

RC: Yes, he found some of his identity there, but the unique thing is that he didn't give Israel ultimate value. That's why he turned down the constant temptation to become king, to be a political success. He realized that he could never find ultimate meaning and identity there. Human societies and cultures were too transient. He found his identity in faith in God. He placed his ultimate commitment with the Eternal. Therefore, life was for him a constantly growing, developing pilgrimage of faith.

P: But where's the security? That sounds like an anxious life of risk.

RC: It is indeed a life of adventure and risk. But it surely is no more anxious than trying to preserve

97

yourself in a crumbling and decaying system, when all the customary landmarks are shifting with social and cultural earthquakes.

C: I agree with you, Reverend Carter. After all, there is fulfillment in the pilgrimage itself. Like we say in a lighter context, "getting there is half the fun."

P: Then self-identity is constantly undergoing change?

RC: Yes, I think so. It is my conviction that this very thing was happening with Jesus. He moved from identifying himself as the carpenter-son of Joseph and Mary to the identity of prophet and teacher. But his faith-pilgrimage led him further to identify himself with God, first as his Messiah in a political sense, then finally as God's suffering servant in a deeply religious sense.

C: This is really making sense to me.

P: Yes, but look where it led him—to a cross and a hideous death. The system eventually killed him.

RC: That's true. And to make a play on words, the cross was the crux for him; it was the ultimate crisis, the decisive challenge to his faith-pilgrimage. And this is precisely where his disciples did not understand him. Judas wanted him to lead the revolution and make himself the king by force, to identify himself with the political kingdom of Israel, to assure himself a place in history. But Jesus had passed that point long ago. The sin of Judas was his ultimate commitment to finding his identity in the kingdom of this world and not in the kingdom of God. Jesus had his commitment in the kingdom of God. Judas tried to force him back to the kingdom of men.

C: But that would make Jesus untrue to himself and God. It would deny the direction of his own faith-pilgrimage.

RC: Exactly. And the excruciating thing about it was in his approaching death. He could have copped out, taken a boat for Spain, but that would have been a complete loss of identity.

C: So, to be authentic, he had to carry his convictions to the ultimate—even death.

RC: Right. The ultimate identity crisis for us all is death. We wonder if it is the end, if we will have life in another dimension, if we will retain identity.

P: So Jesus went to the cross to prove himself right.

RC: Not so much that, as to be faithful, to be true to the kingdom of God, to carry out the belief that true identity is only with the eternal, and not with the temporal. Likewise with us, if we are tied to the temporal, we ultimately lose our identity. But if we are committed to the eternal, the temporal crises of identity are only that. We can withstand them because we are not ultimately bound to them.

P: How about Jesus' death?

RC: How about his resurrection? The Good News is that God vindicated him for his faith-pilgrimage. God restored him to life, affirming his identity forever. More than that, he is, says the author of Hebrews, the pioneer and per-fector of our faith-pilgrimage. He blazed a trail for us and helps us complete our journey on it. He wants to bring us to the same full identity that he has with the Father.

P: You believe then that he helps us over the crises and troubles of our times.

RC: Like the gospel says, he helps us even to the point of laying down his life for us. He had to blaze the trail alone, but we have the advantage of his help. He stands by to help us grow, to develop, to come to wholeness. He helps span the chasms of doubt, the turbulences of frustration and defeat, the pain of suffering and death. You might say that he is . . . a bridge over troubled waters.

(Music up, last verse of "Bridge over Troubled Waters." Characters take their leave during the music.)

So Little Time

This sermon is designed for use with a relatively small group
—say, six to thirty persons. Participants are asked to remain
silent throughout, although discussion may be permitted at the
end.

A copy of the front page of the local newspaper is handed to
each person. It has been specially printed to include a detailed
account of the deaths of all those present. An example of such
a printout used with a seminar group is on the next page.
Note the attention to the customary form of disaster announcements.

When those present have had a moment to read the account,
each person is given a copy of the state certificate of death,
properly completed with his own name and basic information.
The leader speaks:

It is amazing how quickly one's physical existence is
wiped out. You have been dead for a week now. At this
very moment people are going through your furniture,
clothing, files, etc., and are sorting them out. What can't
be used will be thrown away. It takes so little time to remove all our belongings. It is as if we never were—except
for the impact our living had on other persons and the
memories they will keep alive.

The Rev. Harold Warlick is minister of Trinity Baptist Church,
Seneca, South Carolina 29678.

TENNESSEAN

NASHVILLE, TENN., MONDAY, OCT. 30, 1972   10 CENTS

2 Hijackings

Eastern Agent Shot to Death At Houston

By KENNETH GEPFERT

MIAMI (AP) — Four armed hijackers, including a father and son wanted on charges of bank robbery and murder forced an Eastern Air Lines jet with 40 persons aboard to Cuba yesterday after killing one man and wounding another in Houston, the FBI said.

Kenneth W. Whittaker, special agent in charge of the FBI in Miami, identified three of the hijackers after interviewing passengers and crew members on the plane's return. The fourth hijacker was not identified.

THE FBI said air piracy warrants were issued for Charles Andrew Tuller, Jr., 49, a former U.S. government employe, salesman and stockbroker; his son, Bryce Matthew Tuller, 19, an electrician's helper, and William Graham, 18, not further identified.

Whittaker said the father and son team attempted to hold up Crystal Plaza Branch of the Arlington Trust Co., in Arlington, Va., last Wednesday. The bank manager and a policeman were killed during the attempted robbery.

The elder Tuller resigned Oct. 18 from a $26,436 a year job as a Commerce Department specialist in promoting minority business affairs, a department spokesman said. The spokesman said Tuller gave "ill health" as his reason for his resignation.

BOND FOR all three hijackers, who were still in Cuba, was set at $1 million by Magistrate H. Lingo Platter in Houston. In addition, the Tullers have been charged with attempted bank robbery, unlawful flight and murder in connection with the bank holdup.

Authorities said Tuller has a

—UPI Telephoto

umly Criticized

attendant Toni Wellons during a press surrounding the hijacking of an Eastern ed and another injured.

---

ission Head ical Conflict

April 27 let-o member of an "hold any tical party or tion."

requested to on campaign

which shed new light on the maneuvering of the state administration in deciding not to hold an election for the vacant seat as required by the state constitution.

Other stipulations, which mean that both sides are in

Entire Vandy Class Killed

NASHVILLE — In perhaps the worst tragedy in recent Nashville history, 20 Vanderbilt students and their professor were killed yesterday afternoon shortly after 4 p.m.

An entire section of the Divinity Quadrangle collapsed.

In the building at the time of collapse were members of a class being taught by Dr. John Killinger. None survived the disaster.

AUTHORITIES traced the collapse to two faulty beams in the building's roof. Mayor Beverly Briley has ordered a full investigation of the accident.

Killinger, a professor of theology and literature, had only recently been appointed a full professor. A prolific writer, he was most noted for his innovative work in the Dean Walter Harrelson expressed his 'shock and grief' at the death of the popular professor and stated that both Killinger and the students will be "sorely missed."

AMONG THE deceased are: Donald E. Bailey of Nashville; James J. Baker of Elwood, Ind.; Jerry Barnes of Shawnee, Okla.; Robert R. Baldwin of Nashville; Harold K. Bales of Nashville; Lawrence H. Balleine of Kewaunee, Wis.; Darrell E. Berger of Oregon, Ohio; Douglas B. Fleeman of Memphis; H. Geraint M. Jones of Nashville; Thomas B. Martin of Nashville; Donald Male of Nashville; Larry B. McNeil of Lufkin, Tex.; James E. McReynolds of Nashville; Timothy D. Murtaugh of Ann Arbor, Mich.; Richard L. Sprague of Seattle, Wash.; Glenn J. Stewart of Lorain, Ohio; Harold Warlick of N. Augusta, S.C.; David L. and Glenda Webb of Nashville.

A memorial service for the class will be held at 10 a.m. Friday in Vanderbilt's Ben'on Chapel. The Rev. Beverly Asbury, university chaplain, and Dr. Frank Gulley will officiate the service.

A memorial fund has been established for the class. Contributions may be sent to Vandy Class Fund, Vanderbilt University.

Wc Ton Say

The New York Times New

WASHINGTO yesterday that the china would not b set by North Vie

However, the mism about an details of the cea

MOREOVER, appearing in a sure North Vietn seeking to rene reached by Hen: Hanoi's chief neg

"Substantiall mered out and t made 'crystal cl can be made fin principal parts of said on "Issues Broadcasting Co.

North Vietna day the details reached by Kissi curity affairs ad member who is tions, insisted th it once indicated

IN PRIVATE said in recent da ing to back awa for a ceasefire chinery for a n

(T

★ ★ ★

Entire Vandy Class Killed

NASHVILLE — In perhaps the worst tragedy in recent Nashville history, 20 Vanderbilt students and their professor were killed yesterday afternoon shortly after 4 p.m.

An entire section of the Divinity Quadrangle collapsed.

In the building at the time of collapse were members of a class being taught by Dr. John Killinger. None survived the disaster.

AUTHORITIES traced the collapse to two faulty beams in the building's roof. Mayor Beverly Briley has ordered a full investigation of the accident.

Killinger, a professor of theology and literature, had only recently been appointed a full professor. A prolific writer, he was most noted for his innovative work in the

Dean Walter Harrelson expressed his 'shock and grief" at the death of the popular professor and stated that both Killinger and the students will will be "sorely missed."

AMONG THE deceased are: Donald E. Bailey of Nashville; James J. Baker of Elwood, Ind.; Jerry Barnes of Shawnee, Okla.; Robert R. Baldwin of Nashville; Harold K. Bales of Nashville; Lawrence H. Balleine of Kewaunee, Wis.; Darrell E. Berger of Oregon, Ohio; Douglas B. Fleeman of Memphis; H. Geraint M. Jones of Nashville; Thomas B. Martin of Nashville; Donald Male of Nashville; Larry B. McNeil of Lufkin, Tex.; James E. McReynolds of Nashville; Timothy D. Murtaugh of Ann Arbor, Mich.; Richard L. Sprague of Seattle, Wash.; Glenn J. Stewart of Lorain, Ohio; Harold Warlick of N. Augusta, S.C.; David L. and Glenda Webb of Nashville.

A memorial service for the class will be held at 10 a.m. Friday in Vanderbilt's Benton Chapel. The Rev. Beverly Asbury, university chaplain, and Dr. Frank Gulley will officiate the service.

A memorial fund has been established for the class. Contributions may be sent to Vandy Class Fund, Vanderbilt University.

We will be dead for a long time.
There are no hidden meanings.
You really don't control anything.

The leader requests that each person close his eyes. Then he says:

There is no particular reason why you lost out on some things. The world is not necessarily just.

Think of the one thing you achieved in life which you are most happy about. Think of the circumstances surrounding it.

Now think about that one piece of unfinished business you regret not having lived long enough to see finished. What will you miss most?

(Pause.)

Our names are printed in the newspaper. We are but mere words among other words. Somehow the other words appear quite foolish beside them.

A tape recording of television commercials is played. It can be made with a cassette recorder and any television set. The commercials are conjoined so that they run continuously, underlining the absurdity and inanity of a materialistic society.

After a few minutes of the recording, the leader says:

Once you're gone, you're gone. Few people receive a chance to start over. I'm glad you're not dead. Life is short. Go forth and live. Tell those people you love that you love them. Involve yourself in that unfinished business. Throw off your confinement and live. Embrace life to its fullest while you have it. Get in touch with your body, your senses, your people, your world. Don't turn your back on love.

The sermon may conclude with a recording of music —perhaps Peggy Lee singing "Is That All There Is?" or Janis Joplin singing "Get It While You Can."

Easter Dialogues I and II

I

Pastor: The Lord be with you.

People: And with you also.

Pastor: Lift up your hearts.

People: We lift them to the Lord.

Pastor: Let us glorify the Lord.

People: For all his goodness to us.

Pastor: What do you know?

People: He is risen from the tomb. Hallelujah!

Pastor: Who is risen from the tomb?

People: The Christ is risen from the tomb! Hallelujah! Praise the Lord!

Pastor: When did he die?

People: Last Friday, about three o'clock in the afternoon.

Pastor: What was the cause of his death?

People: Crucifixion, loss of blood, suffocation, a broken heart, an overdose of our lack of love.

Pastor: How do you know that the Christ is risen from the tomb?

People: Mary Magdalene and the other Mary told Peter

The Rev. Ray Dykes is minister of the First Presbyterian Church, Sparta, Tennessee 38583.

and John, and they told the other disciples, and the disciples told the church, and the church told us.

Pastor: What does all of this have to do with you?

People: We are a part of the Christ. Hallelujah!

Pastor: Then you were once dead?

People: We were as dead as doornails—dead in hate, dead in sin, dead in sorrow, dead in pain.

Pastor: And now you are risen from the tomb?

People: We are alive forevermore. We have come to a newness of life. Hallelujah!

Pastor: Does that mean that you will never again be sad, that you will never again hate or hurt?

People: It means that sadness and hatred and pain will never again defeat us. It means that the victory is always assured.

Pastor: Are you celebrating the victory today?

People: Hallelujah! Amen!

Pastor: What kind of mood are you in?

People: A joyful, excited, happy mood.

Pastor: Then why are you not smiling?

People: It's hard to read and smile at the same time.

Pastor: How do you express your joy?

People: By participating in this service of worship.

Pastor: How else do you express your joy?

People: By answering your questions. May we ask you some questions?

Pastor: You certainly may.

People: What does Easter mean to you?

Pastor: It means I once was lost but now I'm found, was blind but now I see.

People: What else does Easter mean?

Pastor: It means the kingdom of heaven has begun, that

the Messiah has arrived, that sin and death have been defeated, that evil is on its way out, that the Christ lives and reigns, that my eternal life has begun.

People: What can we do to keep Easter going all year round?

Pastor: Live, love, and live in love.

People: What does that mean?

Pastor: It means to be ready and willing to love another and to receive another's love.

People: We love you.

Pastor: And I love you.

People: Are you going to preach a sermon this morning?

Pastor: You and I have just preached a far more eloquent sermon than I could ever preach by myself.

Unison: In the name of the Father, the Son, and the Holy Spirit. Hallelujah! Amen!

II

Pastor: The Lord be with you.

People: And with you also.

Pastor: Lift up your hearts.

People: We lift them to the Lord.

Pastor: Let us glorify the Lord.

People: For all his goodness to us.

Pastor: Why are so many of you here this morning?

People: We want to celebrate the resurrection of the Christ. Hallelujah!

Pastor: Could I persuade you to do your celebrating elsewhere?

People: We think that this is the best place in the world to celebrate the victory of life over death. Praise the Lord!

Pastor: Yes, but you make so much noise when you celebrate, and I was hoping for a nice, quiet service.

People: We're sorry, but the resurrection of the Christ is not something you whisper about.

Pastor: OK, then, what is it that you want to shout?

People: We want to shout, "The Christ is risen from the tomb!"

Pastor: What else?

People: "We came out of that tomb with him!"

Pastor: That doesn't make any sense. Say it so I can understand.

People: We've been saved! Hallelujah!

Pastor: Saved from what?

People: Saved from our sin, our lack of love. Saved from death, despair, spiritual suffering, and inner conflict.

Pastor: I know better than that. You still suffer and despair every now and then.

People: Oh, yes. But we know now that sooner or later our suffering and despair will always be overwhelmed by the spirit of him who gave his life to ransom us.

Pastor: But how do you know that?

People: Because it has already happened to us at least once.

Pastor: You have told me *from* what you've been saved. *To* what are you saved?

People: Saved by his power divine, saved to new life sublime! Praise the Lord!

Pastor: Now you're making altogether too much noise.

People: We make more noise than this watching a football game. It would be a shame to make more noise over a touchdown than over our salvation to new life sublime!

Pastor: Excuse me, but I don't understand this business about "new life sublime."

People: That means that God has helped us as individuals to get ourselves together, to become whole persons.

Pastor: Tell me more.

People: "New life sublime" means that the kingdom of heaven has begun in our lives. It means that by the power of the Holy Spirit we can turn the most terrible situation into a heavenly occasion.

Pastor: How do you do that?

People: By loving God.

Pastor: How do you to that?

People: By loving ourselves and our neighbors equally.

Pastor: I love you.

People: And we love you. Did we do it again?

Pastor: Do what again?

People: Did we help you preach the sermon like we did last Easter?

Pastor: You and I have again preached a far more eloquent sermon than I could have preached by myself.

Unison: In the name of the Father, the Son, and the Holy Spirit. Hallelujah! Amen!

A Christmas Eve Letter

This sermon may be read live by three voices or prerecorded on tape. In either case, certain background effects are considered useful. First, there should be tape-recorded sounds of war—tracer bullets, mortar fire, sporadic bombing, etc. As these noises fade slightly, two scripture verses are read—Isaiah 52:7 and Matthew 5:9. A moment of silence. Then Longfellow's hymn, "I Heard the Bells on Christmas Day," is sung softly in the background while the first letter is read. (If possible, a slight increase in volume occurs when the following words are sung: "And in despair I bowed my head: 'There is no peace on earth,' I said. 'For hate is strong and mocks the song of peace on earth, good will to men.'") The same hymn may be continued during the reading of the second letter, or "Onward, Christian Soldiers" may be substituted. There is no music during the reading of the telegram. At the conclusion, the confessional hymn "Dear Lord and Father of Mankind" may be read or sung by the congregation.

A Christmas Eve Letter

Dear Mom and Dad,

I had thought it would be over by this time. But the war drags on and on. I am writing you on Christmas

The Rev. Jerry L. Barnes is minister of the University Baptist Church, Shawnee, Oklahoma 74801.

Eve because you well know how much this season of "peace" means to me.

The sounds of war are constantly with us. When I look at this scarred and gutted land, I think how ironic it is that the calm and tranquility of this ancient people have been broken, for thousands of mornings, by the clatter of machine guns and the booming of heavy artillery.

On this Christmas Eve I have been trying to sort out the line of an old hymn. For the life of me I can't remember the title, but the words keep going around and around in my mind. They are almost maddening: "In despair I bowed my head. 'There is no peace on earth,' I said. 'For hate is strong and mocks the song of peace on earth, good will to men.' " Those words mix and mingle with all the sounds of war which have lodged in my mind the pathos and tragedy of this terrible insanity.

Dad, how can the two things be reconciled? In this season when I am so thick with emotion, I am trying to sort out some reasons why we do what we do to each other! How do you reconcile the words of Isaiah, "How beautiful upon the mountains are the feet of him who brings good tidings, who publishes *peace*"? Or "They shall beat their swords into plowshares, and their spears into pruning hooks; nation shall not lift up sword against nation, neither shall they learn war any more"? How do we reconcile this war with the saying of Jesus, "Blessed are the peacemakers, for they shall be called the children of God"?

Dad, how do you reconcile that saying with what I experienced last week? Two deaths stood out in the midst of all the others. One was a kid of seventeen from Pennsylvania. The other was an Oriental, not much more than a boy. From where? Who knows? They died a few feet from each other.

When the young kid from Pennsylvania reported for duty to replace our machine-gunner who had rotated home, he was as nervous and scared as he could be. He had lied about his age to enlist in the Army and become a part of this "elite" paratrooper regiment. Here he was! And less than six hours later, he was dying. In that death, which took too long for me, and not long enough for him, I heard him asking the company medic, "How do you die?" Now, how do you reconcile that with those words from the Bible, "nation shall not lift up sword against nation. Neither shall they learn war anymore"?

Then there was the death of the Oriental boy who had been defined as our "enemy." The two had been killed almost back to back. It wasn't until a day and a half later—with a lull in the fighting—that the stench of his death reminded us that we had to dispose of his body. We wrapped him in a poncho and rolled him over the side of the mountain into no-man's land like you would some animal!

Now, every time I look into the nonseeing eyes of that Oriental boy—so full of nothing which keeps saying so much—I want someone to tell me why we define him as "enemy." He looked so innocent and harmless in death. The real question for me on this Christmas Eve is, Who is my enemy? I have begun to suspect everyone! Is the enemy the President, who fears the industrialists? Is it the military leaders who fear for their careers, or the politicians who fear their constituency? Or is the enemy the people back home who fear for the economy?

Dad, I don't mean to show disrespect, but is your job in the munitions plant more important than the lives of these boys? And Mom, is the new home you desire so much really that important? Please ask Jim why he hasn't spoken out against this insanity. I know the university frowns on professors taking controversial stands, but I can't understand his silence.

Who is my enemy? Next Sunday, ask our minister why he hasn't attacked the immorality of this savage conflict. Is it because the membership of the church is so dependent on the war economy?

Maybe I'm my own enemy. I have not had the courage to lay down my weapons and walk away from this insanity. I suppose the tragedy of the whole war is that many of us are unwilling to suffer the consequences of a courageous act!

Sometimes I don't know what to think. Maybe it's better not to think too much. I am so depressed. I almost wish it weren't Christmas.

I love you. It's getting dark. This is the worst time. Pray for me.

> Your son,
> Joey

A New Year's Eve Letter

Dear Son,

We enjoyed your Christmas Eve letter so much! The weather here is lovely—like spring of the year. Mother and I are glad you are well. You are a good boy to write.

Things go well here. There are nearly eight hundred men at the plant now. That's an increase of three hundred over this time last year. My paycheck has gone up too. It's a good thing, what with the new house and all. God has been good to us!

Our minister reminded us of our blessings last Sunday by preaching a strong sermon on patriotism and how righteousness exalteth a nation. He's a good man, Son. He was saying, "If we do our part, God will do his!" When he finished, we sang "Onward, Christian Soldiers." Mother and I were proud to think of you over there fighting for us.

Keep up the good work. And hurry home. Your new room is waiting! Write soon.
                    Love,
                        Dad and Mother

Telegram

                        Department of Defense
                        The Pentagon
                        Washington, D.C.
                        April 5, 1972

Mr. and Mrs. Joseph Kowalski, Sr.
1501 South Oklahoma
Hastings, Nebraska

Dear Mr. & Mrs. Kowalski, Sr.:

We regret to inform you that your son, Sgt. Joseph Kowalski, Jr., was killed in the line of duty on April 1, 1972.

You can be proud of your son who gave his life for such a noble cause. Please accept the sympathy of the Department of Army for his death.
Cordially,

Secretary of Army

The Colors of Worship

This sermon was originally recorded on tape for use in Lenten services. The text was read in a pleasant baritone voice at a moderate pace and with rich pauses throughout. Various sound effects, as well as musical cues, are indicated beside the script. On one occasion colored lights were used in addition to the tape recording, but several persons who heard the recording with and without lights said that the imagistic quality of the language was more vivid without them.

Music cue:
"Theme" from
Shaft

Metronome

There are colors in worship
The paraments
The stoles, stained-glass windows
Tell a color story
A story of time
Moving on
Unfolding
An event. . .

Music cue:
"Somewhere, over
the Rainbow"
(fadeout)

There are colors in worship

Dr. Gary M. Jones is minister of the Hillwood Presbyterian Church, Nashville, Tennessee 37205.

Metronome

Green grow the rushes, ho!
On the other side of the fence!
Green is the color of my true love's hair
And the marshes of Glynn
Lanier said so, and why should a poet
   be wrong?
Green was Wordsworth's color
And remember how Lady Chatterley
   and her
Gamekeeper lover tangled in the rain.

Effect: Summer
       rainstorm
       (fadeout)
Metronome

Green is jealous—like poison, man!
Eating out the heart of the insecure,
   uncertain lover!
It is the excrescent bile of death and
   has
the smell of putrefaction.
It is the stagnant stillness of the weed-
choked, algae-ridden pond
The mother lode of mosquito-ridden
   palaces.
Green is the Spirit color!
Holy! Holy! Holy! Green nada of hosts!
The long holy season full of
liturgy and the green—surplice,
collar, dossal—hanging, just
hanging there limp

117

Not alive—limp—lifeless—not
fruitbearing—still, still as the
shading limbs of the evergreen juniper
   bush—

Green, a brocaded background hung
near an altar, symbolizing life—
but hanging, hanging. . . .

If a man had green hair he would be *so*
   different—
He would be fool, be clown, be jester

Effect:
   Laughter
   (*fadeout*)

Laughed at, ridiculed, scorned, jeered
   at!
Just think! Green hair could
produce all that!
Even a Cross—if there's enough
   hatred of green—

Oh! But everybody loves the long
   green.
She comes undulating her sensual way
into the awareness—she seduces
me with her allure.
Her potential—her green potential—!
Everyone has his price.
Oh you long green Judas Fruit!—Las
   Vegas, here I come!

Music cue:
   "Red Sails
   in the Sunset"

118

or
"Sunrise, Sunset"

Red sails in the sunset! Red
is dead!
Red lipstick!
Everyone knows that to see red is
to stop!
Slam on the brakes!
Stop!
Stop what?
You embarrass me!
My face is red!
Drop dead!
You said—Red!
Whassa madder you a bloody commie?
Oughter kill them commie bastards!
Kill 'em! Use napalm, defoliant,
Nuclear war heads! The lot!

Effect:
Gunfire
(*fadeout*)

Let the blood run, man!
Blood!
Gory, running, slippery blood
pulsing out of pierced arteries . . .
and wounds. . . .
Calvary wounds. . . .
Something poured out of the Man's
side . . . .
That's a bloody thing, that. . . .
Knocking off a guy that wasn't red—
Spreading a man on a cross—
A gory thing!
Love, agape, started out gory!
Yea—Red, scarlet, rosy-colored.

The color of importance to church,
and Christian . . .

Does it mean bleed a little?
A lot?

Metronome

Black is beautiful
Black is death, darkness, all over the
  face of the earth. . .
Black is gloomy, despondent,
The color of depth, of caves, of holes
  in the ground . . .
Black is the funeral parlor
And the sounds of Digger O'Dell-l-l
Black is the rending time
When veils are torn in two
And despoiled, desperate, abused
  faces raise their anguish
In the cry of "Overcome!"
Black is the color of cause
Martin Luther King,
Eldridge Cleaver, Rap Brown,
  Angela Davis, Malcolm X,
Muhammed Ali, Rufus Scott
and Leona
"Do you love me?"
Black Muslim,

Music cue:
  "When the
  Saints Go
  Marching In"

Ragtime, Jazz, New Orleans
And the Blues,
    Summertime

  (*fadeout*)

120

But livin' ain't easy
When you're black
  And isolated, lonely,
    put down, mistrusted,
In your place. . . . .
Black is the color of my true
    friend's hair, face, hands

Metronome

He's my brother. . . .

Purple is a people eater
The color of majesty
Worn by kings and courtiers
The robes of royalty.
Purple is bruises
  The boxer, the wrestler,
    the soccer player's shin
Purple is the color of Lent
    the color of getting ready for Easter
  And giving up something
  Self-denial. . . .
Purple is apoplexy,
  The hue of man's reaction to change
  To alteration, to the challenge
Of taking another look at the
  Way he feels, he acts, or doesn't!
Purple is the violet
  And the iris with its velvet
    arrogance in the caressing wind. . . .
Purple is a song

Music cue:
  "When the
  Deep Purple
  Falls"

121

(fadeout)

When the deep purple falls. . . .
the dulcet tone of the Crosby, Harry
    James,
Sinatra era—
Purple is the color of words
    written in mockery
    "This is Jesus
    King of the Jews"
    In several languages. . . .
Purple is a king's name

Metronome

White is the hue of purity
The color of the Easter lily
And its message of hope, of triumph
Of stones rolling away,
Of empty borrowed tombs in
forgotten graveyards.
White is apartheid
And minority—although
in the driver's seat. . . .
White is blank paper
Nothing without the poet's
    sensitivity
And the prose writer's insight.
White is unprinted newsprint
With nothing to say
    No murders
    No rapes
    No advertisements
    Nothing . . . .
White is the linen of my marriage bed

122

The color of my bride's sacrificial gown
The cake. . . the candles. . . the face
of the groom.

Music cue:
"Here Comes
the Bride"

(fadeout)

White is sandwich bread,
    fish meat,
Mashed potatoes
And a formal shirt to go with tux.
White is hope
The unblotted chapter of tomorrow
And tomorrow and tomorrow

There is a rainbow
A sign in the sky
A year of color
    of liturgy
As one season becomes another
It takes all colors—
And when they run together
It is the Easter Season—White
All colors in one
All together
All pure
All joined.
A rainbow of hope. . . .

There are colors in worship

Music cue:
"Reveille"

123

A Parable of Life

This sermon, designed as a "participation event," was used with a group of about twenty persons. Chairs were arranged in a circle. On the floor in the middle of the circle was a baby blanket, and, on the blanket, a six-month-old child, Jason Sprague.

The congregation was instructed that it should remain silent, but that any form of participation other than speaking was permitted. Two tape recorders, at alternate ends of the room, carried the text of the sermon. There were large chunks of silence on the tapes, however, filled only by the noises of the child and of the movements of participants.

The script of the recordings is reproduced here. What happened during the sermon cannot be reproduced except in the form of a few impressions. But first, the script:

Tape (child's voice): My name is Jason! I define a small portion of the stream of life. There is something very special about me; I am different from every other living creature in the whole world. I am I. I experience different kinds of body activities. I suffer, I enjoy, and in lots of ways I announce to the world that I am here. I am a center of thought, feeling, action, and desires in

The Rev. Richard Sprague is minister of the Lobelville United Methodist Church, Lobelville, Tennessee 37097.

relationship. I would like you to spend the next few minutes sharing in my life.

(Silence.)

Tape (adult's voice): "The spirit of God has made me, and the breath of the Almighty gave me life." (Job 33:4 RSV)

(Silence.)

Tape (mother's voice, reading from *The Prophet,* by Kahlil Gibran):

"Your children are not your children.
They are the sons and daughters of Life's longing for itself.
They come through you but not from you,
And though they are with you yet they belong not to you.
You may give them your love but not your thoughts.
For they have their own thoughts. You may house their bodies but not their souls,
For their souls dwell in the house of tomorrow, which you cannot visit, not even in your dreams.
You may strive to be like them, but seek not to make them like you.
For life goes not backward nor tarries with yesterday."

(Silence.)

Tape (adult's voice): To participate in the life of another human being is to discern sanctity in existence and in the human enterprise. It is to know the worth of being alive as a person. To participate in the life of another human being is to accept the gift of life and to

125

celebrate the gift of one's own uniqueness as a human being.

(*Silence.*)

Tape (adult's voice): These few moments of participation in a life were for those who see miraculous sights and envision all of the wonders hidden from the eye. It was for those who hear multitudinous sounds and listen to the symphonies that silence brings. To participate in the life of another human being is to worship the God of life.

Jason was an arena of the raw forces coming to shape in a young life. He gurgled, cooed, rolled over, pushed up on his hands, looked around at the strange people.

The group watched—and listened.

After a few minutes he began to push up, then tumbled over the edge of the blanket onto the hard floor. This annoyed him and he would cry or whimper.

One man rose and picked him up and set him back on the blanket.

This was repeated several times, with various participants involved in replacing him.

Once his shoe fell off. A man picked him up and held him in his lap while another man came over, knelt, and replaced the shoe. The first man took the baby's hand and reached out to muss the hair of the second.

Another time, someone present sat on the edge of the blanket and played with some plastic keys on a chain to amuse the child.

The parents of the child never moved to rescue him or

to make him comfortable. His mother later confessed that it was extremely difficult not to do so. "I wanted to go around afterwards," she said, "and write down the names of all the ones who went to help my baby."

In the discussion following the "sermon" a minister who was present said that the time had had a great effect on him. He had just come from a rest home where he had called on a woman who was bedridden with arthritis.

"Her whole body was wracked with pain," he said. "She even had arthritis in one eye. And the medicine they were giving her had caused an ulcer in the other eye. She was all drawn up in a knot, and her hands were curled up like claws. If they give her enough medicine to stop the pain, it will kill her."

He had asked, before leaving, whether it would hurt her if they held hands to pray. He grasped those useless hands, he said, and they prayed.

This man was the first to go to the baby when he rolled off the blanket. His mind was a muddle of contrasts—the poor woman and this healthy infant.

Others spoke of the guilt they had felt in not going to the baby's aid, yet the hesitance they felt about going. Some were not parents and confessed that they did not know what to do with a baby.

One or two alluded to the way they had meditated on the child's innocence and inexperience, and how it put into noticeable contrast their own involvements in life, disillusionments, and implication in the collective guilt of man.

As the group disbanded, one young man, a hippie, said to the child's father, "That shook me up more than anything I can remember." "He was deeply moved," said the father, "he meant it positively."

A Pantomime Sermon

The stage is dark, and in the darkness the congregation sits listening to a recording of the Beatles' "Let It Be." Toward the end of the recording the lights slowly come up to reveal three figures center stage. The figure in the middle is bearded, wears a white robe, and is slightly reminiscent of Jesus. Throughout most of what happens he remains calm and patient with the other two people. They are a man and a woman, both dressed in rather neuter fashion, wearing black trousers and jerseys. The two of them look at Jesus with some puzzlement and then at each other. Then an idea is born. They exit and bring in a box of props.

They take out a Bible and place it in Jesus' hand in the style of Billy Graham. One of them manually forces Jesus' mouth into a toothy grin. They both occupy themselves with the task of "radiating warmth" and handing out leaflets while the sound of "Let It Be" is heard at a faster speed. But they grow disenchanted with this and it shows in their faces.

A second idea. They take away the Bible and pull out

Mr. James Baker is a student at Vanderbilt Divinity School, Nashville, Tennessee 37240.

berets and rifles. A black beret is put on Jesus, along with a bandolier and a rifle. "Let It Be" is played along with extremely passionate and martial music while the man and woman pantomime a struggle against fascist/communist forces. Slowly disenchantment sets in once again.

They then turn to introspection. Jesus is dressed as a Viennese psychoanalyst with pince-nez and notebook and pencil. The man and woman lie down on either side of him and simultaneously pour out their lives. However, they do not actually speak; they are pantomiming two tapes played at a rapid speed so that all we can hear is gibberish. During this the record chants over and over one line from the song, "There will be an answer." But this leads to nothing.

They both get up and dress Jesus once again. They give him a guitar and perhaps place a flower in his hair. One of them raises his arm and forces his fingers to form the peace sign. The record is played once again and the two dance to "Jesus' music." The sound of the phonograph needle running wild across the record is heard, and once again the idea is seen to have been fruitless.

Next they dress Jesus in a clown's hat and paint rosy cheeks on him and on each other. They skip about tossing confetti in the air, blowing up balloons, and clanging cymbals to the music, which is once again played at a fast speed. The recording slowly winds down, as do the man and the woman. They let go their balloons, which fizzle off to die, and they pelt Jesus with confetti in disgust.

Finally Jesus calmly arises. He washes the paint from the cheeks of all three of them and they are returned to their appearances in the beginning. Then Jesus slowly and calmly walks down the aisle and out of the building. The man and the woman are left standing, the floor covered with the discarded props—confetti, balloons, hats, etc. They watch him leave, puzzled yet trying to reflect deeply upon what has happened to them.

They slowly turn to one another and there is silence. They stare at one another and then cautiously move toward each other. There is a long hesitant period; perhaps they are looking at each other in depth. Then slowly but determinedly they pull markers from their pockets. With the actions of artists, they begin to correct the flaws in each other. He makes her mouth over, and she redoes his eyebrows. He paints her cheeks and she draws a mustache on him. It is evident that they are making each other grotesque. As the lights dim, the music comes up in the background, "Let It Be."

Lenten Nursery Rhymes

Here we are Lord—your not-too-humble servants
    your beloved prodigals
Here we present to you these scrawny bodies of ours
    these blobs of clay
    these hunks of dirt
Here we offer to you our garbled words
    our pantomimed acts of love
      our frustrated motives
        our confused emotions

Hickory, Dickory, Dock
The mouse ran up the clock
The clock struck one
    Tick—tock . . .
      The clock ticks . . .
              Time stops.

Life praises its Lord.
    Like a magnificent carousel,

The Rev. Raymond Council is Chaplain of the Tennessee Reception and Guidance Center for Children, 2700 Heiman Street, Nashville, Tennessee 37208.

Life praises its Lord.
    By its movement and mystery
    By its beauty and goodness
Life praises its Lord.
And Creation . . .
        fragmented and partial . . .
      groans out that praise
        as it reaches for
        as it stretches towards
      its fullness and completion.
Hickory, Dickory, Dock
The mouse ran up the clock
    Tick—tock . . .
      The clock ticks . . .
                    Time stops.

Let us worship the Lord of our living
    by our kneeling, standing, lying
Let us worship the Lord of our living
    by our praying, singing, screaming
Let us worship the Lord of our living
    by our working, weeping, dancing
Let us worship the Lord of our living
    before our living is snuffed out by the grave,
the dark,
    frightening,
      final,
        finishing,
          not-too-distant grave.
Let us worship the Lord of our living
    by that most significant of human acts—
                         our dying.
For the dust of our living comes upon us

as a hammer upon an anvil.
The grass withers
              The flower fades.
  Hickory, Dickory, Dock
  Tick—tock
      The clock ticks . . .
                    Time stops.

In the land of Nod between
                    the "once upon a time"
                              and
                    the "happily ever after"
We waste our chance to live
We lose our lives
              never to find them again!

Mary had a little lamb,
little lamb, little lamb,
Mary had a little lamb . . .
  Mary had . . .
              O Lamb of God that takest away
the sin of the whole world, have mercy upon us
              O Lamb of God that takest away
the sin of the whole world
              O Lamb of God save us from . . .
ourselves.
  Or is it possible that we have gone too far?
    Is the hour too late this time?
Hickory, Dickory, Dock
  Tick—tock
      The clock ticks . . .
                    Time stops.

133

Indeed, there is no balm in Gilead.
O savagely slain and slaughtered
O savagely slaughtered and slain
    Lamb of God,
                save us from ourselves.
Hollow laughs
    like faked coughs
        communicate more than words.
Forced smiles
    camouflage, cover, conceal
                genuine feelings.
Dry tears
    parched by too many infidelities.
Barren relationships
    soured by too many betrayals.
Mary had a little lamb, little lamb. . .
    O Lamb of God, save us from ourselves.

People no longer read each other.
Everyone crouches
                huddles
                    behind false greetings
                    fraudulent frowns
                    deceptive sweetness.
Our commerce with each other is like that of
    the carpenter building the gallows
                and
    the man sentenced to die.
People live . . . isolated,
    separated,
      alienated.
Confined to
                imprisoned in ourselves
We no longer hunger,

thirst,
  ache,
    for that tender,
      gentle dealing with others.
Nothing is given of ourselves but the residue
                     the remainder
                     the leftover
  and even that is given
  grudgingly, unwillingly.

Humpty-Dumpty sat on a wall.
Humpty-Dumpty had a great fall.
All the King's horses and
All the King's men
Couldn't put Humpty together again.
  Behold the God!
    Yahweh the Life-Giver
    Elohim the Lord
              declaring,
              decreeing
              that life be . . . lived!
  Behold the man!
    imago Dei
    tiller of the land
Hickory, Dickory, Dock
The mouse ran up the clock.
The clock struck one.
  Tick—tock
    The clock ticks . . .
                  Time stops.
  Fugitives fleeing from our acquittal
  Earthen vessels worn and torn
    broken and shattered

135

Until the Second Adam.
O savagely slain and slaughtered
O savagely slaughtered and slain
    Lamb of God,
                save us from ourselves.
  Somewhere in
              our dependent infancy
                 or
              our trembling adolescence
  We stopped.
    Growth came to a screeching halt.
  Time piled upon time
  Illusions scraped upon illusions
  Fantasies heaped upon fantasies
Now I lay me down to sleep
I pray the Lord my soul to keep
If I should die . . .
              before I live
Hickory, Dickory, Dock
  Tick—tock
    The clock ticks . . .
             Time stops.

  Lord, have mercy upon us.
  Christ, have mercy upon us.
  Lord, have mercy upon us.

Jack and Jill went up the hill
To fetch a pail of water . . .
  Jack and Jill went up the hill . . .
  Jack and Jill went . . . . .
  Jack went up the hill
Christ went up the hill
  ascended Golgotha

climbed to the Skull
Christ went up the hill
  and there
    with a beggar and a peddler
      cared.
And his caring stormed the human bastille
  freed men from the enclosures in which they lived
  broke down the barriers they had erected
Christ went up the hill
                          and there suspended
                            between a peddler
                                and
                              a beggar
invited men
            to live
              to breathe
                to love
                  to serve
                    to die with him.
O savagely slain and slaughtered
O savagely slaughtered and slain
    Lamb of God,
                    save us from ourselves.

Jack and Jill went up the hill
To fetch a pail of water.
Jack fell down and broke his crown
  Jack fell down and broke his crown
  Jack fell down . . .
    Christ fell down
  Fell down and got up
  got up and fell down
  fell down and got up

137

got up on a cross
a cross a cross
got up on a cross
and died.
His crimson body
crinkled like crushed foil . . .
His energy fizzled
His vitality gone
His strength dwindled
Nothing left
Everything exhausted
Everything expired
Everything given . . . unflinchingly . . .
O savagely slain and slaughtered
O savagely slaughtered and slain . . .
Hickory . . .
Dickory . . .
Dock . . .
Time . . .
stops.

Jack be nimble
Jack be quick
Jack jump over the candlestick.
And they who dwell in darkness
have seen a great light—
blinding,
illuminating
energizing,
revealing the darkness.
And what is man that the Lord of all creation
should care for him?
But the Lord of creation has clothed his children—

 white skin
  black skin
   red skin
    yellow skin
And loved them—
 loved them—Protestant, Catholic, Jew
 loved them—secretary, banker, farmer
loved them,
 redeemed them,
   healed them.
Jack be nimble
Jack be quick
 And who are we that the Lord of all creation
   should care for us?
But the Lord of creation has loved us—
   our shabby lives
   our desperate lives
   our lonely lives
   our sterile and impotent lives . . .
loved us,
 redeemed us,
  healed us.

O savagely slain and slaughtered
O savagely slaughtered and slain
  Lamb of God,
     save us from ourselves.

Save us by your love—free,
   uncommon,
    very real,
     really real.
Save us by your love—unfeigned,
   enduring,

compelling,
profound.
With such a love now haunt us
tug at us
pull at us
seek us out
seize us.
With such a love now nag us
gnaw at us
hound us
baffle us
emancipate us.

For this is how we end . . .
For this is how we end . . .
not with a shout
or
a whimper
But with the prayer of a man
who loved us—
"Father, forgive them."

Sermon in the Form of a Fable

On the text Mark 10:43 RSV

"It shall not be so among you; but whoever would be great among you must be your servant, and whoever would be first among you must be slave of all."

Dramatis Personae

A and B—professors, members of the Society of Social
      Scientists
M and N—members of the Methodist Monks
S—a Strength Corps volunteer
T—an official in the State Department
STRENGTH—Supplementary Technical Resources En-
      tering National Government to Help

ACT I   The Society of Social Scientists
Early Summer, 1980

A: How much gasoline does it take?

B: A two-quart milk carton would be plenty—you have to

Dr. William A. Beardslee is professor of religion, Emory University, Atlanta, Georgia 30322.

pour it over yourself pretty carefully, though. With milk cartons we could get a group assembled and everyone could do it at once before anyone could stop us.

A: True—but it just isn't the right way. Doing it that way says something, but not just the right way. And I have a better way—one that also comes out of the Eastern tradition of self-sacrifice.

B: Well, you may be right and I want to hear about it, but the Society of Social Scientists never was strong on the aesthetic effect. After all, our Society was founded only five years ago, in 1975, when all at once the tremendous threat of the misuse of social science came over the profession. It was like the sudden reaction of the Atomic Scientists in 1945. Leading social scientists banded together to form a society of social concern—the Society of Social Scientists.

And now a special committee is dealing with the crisis in Brazil. Somehow we have to make clear, no matter what the cost to ourselves, that the crisis in Brazil needs a free and open discussion, and not a manipulated one. It is our issue because our scientific analysis of motivation and of persuasive techniques gives the government what is really a new weapon. Well, you know all this anyway, and we've decided that a group of a thousand social scientists will make this costly gesture to shock the public and the government, to set up an inescapable challenge on the issue of a human discussion of the war in Brazil.

A: I am with you there, and we don't need to go into all this historical background now. Here we are, supporting a very rigid regime in Brazil and the country is just bubbling with unrest and full of Chinese too. It sure looks as if

142

we are on the edge of making a major military investment there, and the power of modern scientific propaganda has grown so fast that the Society of Social Scientists just has to make a protest.

But the gasoline-burning just isn't right. And there is a much better way. Listen to this. The Democratic National Convention will be meeting in Atlantic City in August, and their policy is the one that matters. Just when the convention is acting on this question, a thousand social scientists will line themselves up spaced along the boardwalk at intervals about a rod apart—you remember what a rod is, an English measure used back before we shifted to metric—and while a group presents our protest these men will just quietly walk out into the sea. A few deep-sea lead sinkers in our pockets is all the equipment it will take.

B: A march to the sea, eh? Mm—I see—yes, it is better than the gasoline. But do you really think we can get the group to carry it off? The whole idea is so foreign to our Western tradition.

A: Of course it is a cultural borrowing, and of course it gives suicide an entirely different value from what it usually has in our culture. Japanese women walking into the sea at Saipan in 1944, singing as they walked, is what gave me the idea. But everything points to our needing a sharp change, and the situation is stretched so tight that it can become a vehicle for a new meaning of sacrifice—new, that is, in our Western style of life.

B: You know that we have already decided that most of the group have to be established men, full professors and top-grade industrial research men. Such a radical shift doesn't come easy to them.

143

A: Do you suppose that is why the project has such strong support from the younger men, by the way? Think of all the vacancies it will create!

B: On the contrary, we have had to fight to keep the younger men out and prove that the protest is a solid, mature voice of the Society of Social Scientists.

A: Yes, I am in sympathy with that, but we need to keep it open to the younger men too. The whole point is to create a new dimension of service—not in despair and bitterness, but as a full, whole acceptance of sacrifice. Somehow the sea has much more of that about it than the other way.

B: All right, Atlantic City in August. Of course, no one can say anything to anyone—not even their wives. But the men will be there—you wait and see—and what they do will speak in a way that has to be heard.

ACT II The Methodist Monks
Fall, 1980

M: The Society of Social Scientists—who would have thought it of them? Well, what they did certainly brought about what they wanted—a full and open discussion of the civil war in Brazil and our part in it.

N: Yes, they made quite a splash all right. They planned to have a thousand—948 showed up, but eight of those only waded in in a half-hearted way. And the lifeguards pulled out 22, and some 32 others came to after prolonged artificial respiration. Still and all, it was on its own basis a magnificent success—886 social scientists mostly well-known, established men, joining together in a common act of self-sacrifice. No doubt the tropical storm that after-

144

noon added a lot to the success of the project—the beach was practically deserted at the time, and there was a heavy sea running—otherwise, no doubt, people would have pulled a lot of them out.

M: Well, wouldn't you have tried to?

N: Of course I would, but I respect their stance—a strange mixture of action and passivity, of nonviolent force, to express in the passive act of walking into the sea a passionate desire to change things, to put their hand on the wheel of history. Somehow I have a feeling that in a sense they are more alive now than when they were teaching their classes.

M: Something tells me that their act of service, of self-sacrifice, is gnawing on you because you see that they have captured the public imagination in a way that we never have. The Methodist Monks—that's a nickname people gave us because our group got started back in the late 1960's at some small Methodist university in the southeast, I forget the name—stands for a more continuing style of self-sacrifice—at least I believe it does—and I see a lot of self-projection in the act of the social scientists.

N: Yes, of course I agree that a one-shot act like their walking into the sea is precisely what our style of life has tried to go beyond. And you can see already that some of us have been able to come into the aftermath of this situation in a constructive way that hardly anyone else has been able to. One group of us has been counseling with many of the widows of the social scientists and with the ones who didn't make it on the beach. They really feel guilty. And our freedom from involvement with the project, and yet our common concern, has really helped—they have been free to see something through us that they couldn't see otherwise. And the public has too. I think it is not unimportant that our group in Brazil is the only one, besides the Friends Service Committee, that is able to minister to refugees on both sides of the conflict. But it does bother me that what we can do always seems to be a business of coming in afterward, when things have gone wrong, and working at picking up the broken pieces.

M: Picking up the broken pieces—maybe you put it a little strongly, but it's true that any radical disengagement from the power structure is bound to take away some of your initiative, unless you are an outright revolutionary and succeed in building up a new power structure. So I'll have to go along with you and say that that's exactly what we can expect to be doing always—picking up the broken pieces. It's just because there will always be broken pieces to pick up that there will always be a vocation to step aside from the conventional pattern and be free and ready, as we try to do.

N: I guess you're right, and perhaps I came into the Methodist Monks with some confusion in my mind between the radical and the revolutionary. If we really are radical in our disengagement from the power structure, we can't be effective revolutionaries—we pick up the action on the second beat, to try to deflect and repair something that someone else has started.

M: Exactly. That is the function of service in the world —not to run it, but to be sensitive to the places where it is badly out of order and to try to step in and see that things don't go completely to pot. One thing we are more realistic about than a lot of earlier intentional communities is that we don't think that a radical commitment to service is necessarily going to be a public success. Most of life runs on quite different principles than service, and has to. But we find that some people need a vocation of freedom for service, and we try to provide a pattern of flexibility and openness exactly to those places where, as you put it, someone has to step in and pick up the broken pieces. Take the present furor over the Society of Social Scientists—no one else much was able to *listen*, really listen, to what they were trying to say. If we hadn't been able to interpret it, the result could have been just the opposite of what they intended—you know how resentful most of the churches were at their new statement of the theme of sacrifice, and you know how threatened most professors were by what they did.

N: I suppose that I was attracted into the Methodist Monks partly by the idea that if only someone would give some real, earnest attention to the trouble spots in our society, things would finally begin to get better—but as it is, there just keep on being more trouble spots.

M: Actually, you are just like a lot of our members. The idea of progress is hard to get rid of for most Americans. And it is sobering to find out that total immersion in the life-style of disengagement and service often means less effectiveness. Still, all that doesn't change the validity of ours as one style of vocation—a disciplined group of laymen accepting a common rule of life and spending three months of the year in one of our retreat communities and free to spend up to three other months of the year in the particular tasks of the servanthood that each year calls for. That is our pattern, and the economics of the affluent society make it possible to do it and still bring up families that aren't disadvantaged—let's admit that. After all, one of the glaring gaps of Protestantism is the lack of disciplined patterns of life outside the conventional, and Catholic patterns are awfully medieval —nearly all of our group are married.

N: Yes, and one great thing about it is that so many different religious groups are represented in it. I must say I really felt good the day we got the blessing of the Catholic Bishop McNulty and the Methodist Bishop Boozer.

ACT III The Strength Corps
Winter, 1981

S: Since I came to Washington, I have really been surprised at the way they let us Strength Corps volunteers really come into sensitive areas in the government.

T: In the State Department we have had some pretty sharp debates on whether to do this or not. Even now, after the program has been going on since 1972, we still argue about it. What really amazed me was that they ever passed the law in the first place, but old Nixon was awfully stubborn when he got an idea, and he finally pushed it through.

S: Well, it really was a great idea to let volunteers have a part in responsible work for the government. The Peace Corps model applied to the domestic scene was OK, and Vista was a real challenge. But in a more technically developed society like ours there are other kinds of openings for two-year volunteers, and the terribly understaffed state of so many government departments gave the opportunity for the Strength Corps.

T: You know, one of the real, real interesting things about the Strength Corps is the selection of the volunteers. One of the big ideas of the program is to bridge the generational gap between young, freewheeling idealists like you and people who are established in the structure of society like myself. I wonder whether you **think** the program really means anything along that line or not?

S: Of course, you know that working with guys like you often strains our tolerance as far as it can go. About 15 percent of the Strength Corps volunteers transfer into the Peace Corps each year—you know that.

T: I thought that was because in Washington they couldn't wear blue jeans.

S: Come on. All we want to know is whether you are for real or not. We can see that the social scientists were real at Atlantic City. We can even see that the Methodist Monks are real, and you'd be surprised how many young people have been attracted into the Methodist Monks. There is something real about their combination of discipline and freedom—lots of us have come to see that discipline goes with freedom, from the model of their life, even if we don't go for it ourselves. But here you sit in an office and write memoranda—sometimes read books—talk with someone else in the Department —once in a while take a trip to Costa Rica or someplace —is that for real or not? That's what I'm trying to find out.

T: Well, in the last month or so I haven't had much time to think about whether I'm for real or not. Teddy Kennedy's first term just ran out, and things have hardly shaken down yet—but at any rate the administration is really trying to face up to the fact that the period when the U.S.A. was the greatest power is over.

S: That is pretty tough for the average voter to take. Of course that's why public opinion is so touchy about the situation in Brazil. Lots of people think we've got to be the first power or nothing.

T: Of course the exact figures are hard to get, but China is now producing just about as much as we are, and in ten to fifteen years it will be producing as much as the United States and Russia combined, at its present rate of expansion. This is hard for the American people to realize, even though studies of economic growth showed this was very possible as long as fifteen years ago. Some of the most brilliant empires have been the most short-lived, and the United States is in that class. Our period of being the world's greatest power hasn't lasted as long even as Nebuchadnezzar's Neo-Babylonian Empire—and you know from your college course in religion how short that was.

S: Well, we have a little breather, anyhow. The Chinese are still working hard in Brazil, but the very fact that they have a big industrial plant makes them a little less trigger-happy.

T: And our closing down our section on rationalized motivation analysis and propaganda control, which we did after all those social scientists committed suicide—closing down that department surprisingly enough has given us a fresh start at talking things through in Brazil in quite a human way. At least we're not planning to blow each other to bits over Brazil for the next few months.

S: Yes, you can always argue about what might have been, but in terms of what actually happened, the protest of the social scientists really changed things.

T: They did all right, but don't forget how the public resentment swelled up at first and almost pushed us the other way into a full-scale war. It was only after the first wave of reaction, when some other members of their group began to speak up, and some other people like the Methodist Monks began to speak for them, that what they were saying really began to come through, and the tide of opinion shifted. And don't forget that there had to be some responsiveness here too. The government is not *just* giving in to pressure. People here are trying to exercise their responsibility too. Some of us had actually been plugging away at this same problem behind the scenes for a long time.

S: You really believe that, don't you—that the most effective form of service is just plugging away within the existing structure, making a push for something new once in a while and most of the time just doing what the job calls for.

T: Let's not say the most effective form of service—let's say the one an awful lot of us are called into. And when you think of it, this shift we're going through into the position of a second-rate power is going to take a lot of people who are willing to step in and try to hold things on an even keel, just so we make the shift without blowing everyone to bits. Keep watching us and you may see that our style of service has its freedom and its risks too.

S: You know, our time is up and our author hasn't given us time to say anything about *why* people get involved in trying to be of service—what drives them to it—to what extent it's guilt—to what extent it's self-fulfilment—where the undergirding element of faith in God comes in, and Christ as the Servant.

T: Well, our author thinks a sermon is like an iceberg, as Heinrich Ott says, and there's a lot under water that doesn't show holding up the iceberg that shows. At least we can hope the iceberg won't sink. Hold it a sec while I take the phone. Hello—oh—Mr. Secretary. Yes? What the hell did I mean in that memorandum on Brazil? You say you're about ready to let me go? Mr. Secretary, let me come up and give you some of the backup data on that memorandum, OK? Mr. Secretary, I'll be up this afternoon at 3:30.

Well, let's hope that the research you and I did for that memorandum really will back it up—otherwise . . . ?

Too Much Jesus

This "sermon" was never preached from a pulpit. Its author parted company with the congregation he had ministered to for seventeen years and took some time off to look at the church scene in perspective. Yet he could not stop preaching, so he put his sermons into the form of pastoral letters which he mailed, at his own expense, to ministers and laymen alike. At the time when this anthology is being compiled, he is preaching in a pulpit again, this time as interim minister of a church of another denomination, and the pastoral letters don't come as often as they did. But this example suggests the kind of thing that can be done through "unpreached" preaching.

The country is overevangelized. There is too much Jesus around. More than enough Christianity has turned us toward demoralization. As is said, too much of anything is bad. If we could be sufficiently bold about it, and if we were not so commercially involved, not so institutionally fixated, not so sensually satisfied in our pastoral sinecures, we might be capable of admitting that the phenomenon exists: we have oversold the gospel. But not really the gospel. Our business has not

The Rev. William Dixon Gray, a minister of the Presbyterian Church in the United States, is librarian for Children and Youth Services, Tennessee Department of Mental Health, Nashville, Tennessee 37204.

been the gospel. Our business has been selling any phase or aspect of the biblical religion, featuring Jesus always of course, in order to get customers for our churches. Evangelism always is related to the churches. The gospel can never be seen for what it is by itself. We do not allow it to be primarily and necessarily related to the world it was designed to redeem; it is used as a sales pitch by the communities that in the name of Jesus seek to exist for themselves. Churchmen announce a sales meeting, a great conference on evangelism, not to deal with the problem of too much Jesus, not to enact plans for taking down the Jesus signs that no one, from sheer satiety, can see anymore, not to mix up new emetics that might relieve the national overdose of religion, but, doubtless, to harangue and exhort one another to more prodigious deeds in oversupplying the country with more and more Jesus. The best evangelism now is a counterevangelism. Taking his place in the biblical line of great and honest prophets, claiming jealously to be one of them, ready to die with them, Jesus was himself a counterevangelist. Jesus comes upon the scene riding a white horse, not as a salesman, but as Faithful and True, with a sharp sword issuing from his mouth with which to smite the nations. Our cue is to offer ourselves first for judgment.

Jesus didn't want anyone to oversell him. He seemed especially fearful that those he healed would oversell him. He told them and he told those who had witnessed miracles of healing to keep it to themselves; e.g., "And he charged them to tell no one" (Mark 7:36 RSV). Maybe Jesus wanted to be himself. He wanted to be taken for the Word of God, the Anointed of God, the Great Prophet, the Way, the Truth, the Life. He did not want to be taken for one more than usually handy in doing miracles, who could be counted on to supply wine and bread almost any old time, and who had a way of being on hand when something needed fixing, whether it might be an eye, an ear, or even doing something about the weather, as when he calmed a storm. A person would have a hard time insisting on who he really was if the publicity about his miracles got around uncritically. He could be oversold easily. If he got the reputation for getting kids off drugs, helping others to kick booze or sex or whatever it was that bothered them, and made a great many healthy, wealthy, happy, and religious, then he sure would have a hard time trying to get people to understand who he really was and what it was he really wanted to do and see done. Poor Jesus gets used for everything. Maybe that is our trouble.

Jesus did not enlist his disciples from those he healed. You would think these fellows, the ones who could say "He healed me," would have made the best disciples, making up the group that followed Jesus and were his chosen twelve. Yet now it seems that many who are in the Jesus trade are people who can say, "Jesus helped me kick the habit," or "I was a terrible drunk and Jesus saved me," or "I was a successful businessman but Jesus helped me see that my life was aimless and empty." All these guys now become preachers. It seems that the inevitable happy end to the modern testimony is that the fellow heads for the theological seminary, becomes an evangelist, a worker of some sort, in the name of Jesus. And it might be that that is why the Jesus propaganda comes out so much, "Hey, Jesus can do it for you." A trusting look at the Transfiguration story sees Jesus taking only three of his disciples up the mountain

155

with him, and on the way down he tells them to be quiet about what they saw until Jesus' transcendence is revealed in his resurrection. You have to be careful about Jesus.

Jesus left no pattern as to where his favors might fall. He healed and raised the stricken as though haphazardly, as though to show, it might seem, that he was not under obligation to perform in a set manner, or to pay off for anyone's faith and prayers. We see, now and then, answers to prayer that some might regard as the miraculous. But usually these benefits come to those financially able to afford expensive physicians, hospital, and therapy. The poor don't have their prayers answered. The poor, it is said, go to death row for their crimes while the rich employ costly legal counsel and go free. There is a degree of predictability in the way the fortunate receive favors, so that faith as a gambit for dealing with God must be dismissed and abandoned. In his enigmatic way of showing compassion to all sorts of people, without distinction, Jesus makes faith face up bravely to the perplexities of providence.

A Sermon/Script for Reformation Day

Stage is dark. For a few moments one hears monastic-type music, low chanting music from the early centuries of the church. The stage slowly lightens but only enough to reveal shadowy figures dressed in monk's robes. Their hoods obscure their faces. The stage is dominated by a large, ornate purple tapestry hanging from the back center. Chanting and walking in slow procession, the monks carry in various objects such as crosses, chalices, etc., and place them around the tapestry. The chanting should sound especially haunting and otherworldly, as if coming from an echo chamber. Right front light intensifies to show Augustine *who speaks:*

Augustine: We cannot perceive the immutable truth of things unless they are illuminated by a sun. God is the intelligible light in whom and by whom and through whom all those things which are luminous to the intellect are made luminous. God is light!

Mr. Richard Nelson is a student at Vanderbilt Divinity School, Nashville, Tennessee 37240.

(*Light fades on* Augustine. *Elsewhere on the stage*
Anselm *appears deep in thought.*)

Anselm: God is that than which no greater can be
thought. But that than which no greater can be thought
must exist, not only mentally in idea, but also extra
mentally. (*Satisfied*) Therefore God exists, not only in
idea, mentally, but also extramentally!

(*The light fades and* Thomas Aquinas *appears.*)

Thomas Aquinas: In general, we must make a distinction
between what is *per se notum secundum se* and what is
per se notum quod nos. The proposition God exists is a
proposition *per se notum secundum se,* since God's essence is his existence. And one cannot know God's nature, what God is, without knowing God's existence,
that he is; but a man has no·a priori knowledge of God's
nature and only comes to know that God's essence is
his existence after he has come to know God's existence
(*light begins to fade on* Thomas) so that even though
the proposition that God exists is *per se notum secundum se,* it is not *per se notum quod nos.*

(*Throughout the scene monks continue to carry in
articles, the light around the objects and hanging tapestry flickers brightly, and acolyte monks light candles and
wave censers, bowing and prostrating themselves. The music
gradually intensifies. Finally some monks bring in peasants instead of objects and force them to kneel. The
recalcitrant are beaten. Eventually the peasants are
forced to give money, some of which the monks take
and the remainder of which is placed before the altar.
Some of the monks begin to yawn. They stop prostrating themselves and fall asleep. Some continue to bring*

in objects. By now, the stage should be quite filled and the tapestry well hidden. The light fades as the chanting continues very low and far away.

Suddenly a blaze of light as an organist begins to play "A Mighty Fortress Is Our God." Luther leaps on the well-lit stage. He wears a monk's robe but not a hood.)

Luther: Enough of this perverse piety, this monkery! I tell you that all these appendages (points to objects) are not necessary to keep us from God! You have kept these poor people (points to peasants) servile long enough! Every man is a priest! Every man can come directly to God! All of this (points to objects) is of no importance. (A few monks begin to throw things aside, breaking them.) Stop! Orderly, orderly now! We don't need chaos. Many of these are helpful to our worship of God. Only remove those things which stand in the way and are not a help. Yes, yes, that's better. How about that over there, yes, that's it.

(The monks remove their hoods. Many are wearing masks—some comic, some childish and innocent, some grotesque. Some of the monks begin to move objects to the side of the stage. They do this reverently and cautiously lest they break something. Calvin walks sternly onto the stage. Luther sees him and falls silent.)

Calvin: Our friend Luther is too timid. He was a monk too long! These popish paraphernalia are quite unnecessary. Away with them all! They stand in the way of you and God. Therefore they must be destroyed! Away with them!

(The monks begin to break objects and push objects off the stage, both to the side and off the front.)

159

Calvin: That box of whistles (*points to the organ*) has no place in worship. God comes to a man when he sings from his heart, in simplicity.

(*The organ is smashed and chopped apart. The pieces are thrown off the front of the stage as close to the audience as possible. Lights fade.*

Lights come up to reveal people sitting stiffly in rows of chairs. Masks and cowls have been removed and people are in modern dress. They listen to a Preacher before them.)

Preacher: (*with exaggerated sincerity*) The important thing is our relationship to God. Not the paraphernalia of religious rites and dogmatism. We must strip away the unnecessary, we must demythologize our theology so that it will be acceptable to modern man. We cannot demand that a man change his world view. A twentieth-century man is born with a twentieth-century world view. He does not choose it! Are we to deny him a relation with God because we think the form is more important than the content of our faith? We must not be afraid to remove the myths and symbols from our religion in the interest of our fellowmen.

(*People slowly begin to rise and carefully remove the remaining objects from the stage. They put some in trunks and carry the trunks offstage. Larger objects are covered with a white cloth and moved to the edge of the stage. Some people remain sitting, listening to the preacher.*)

Preacher: Remember, as a great theologian reminded us, the Protestant principle, the principle of the Reformation itself, tells us that none of our symbols are ultimate—

160

they only point to the ultimate. Therefore, we must in faith and boldness strip away the myths and symbols that hide the truth. We must lay bare the truth! We have nothing to fear in this, for God is with us.

(*At this point several of the people pull down the last remaining article on stage—the giant purple cloth —revealing a giant hole. Lights begin to fade. The people scream in horror. Some kneel and cry, etc.*)

Preacher: Nothing! Nothing . . . nothing . . . nothing . . . .

Lights go out. Darkness for a few moments. Then, faintly at first, the sound of electronic beeps and blurps. Slowly the stage lights up to reveal a giant card catalogue filling the back center of the stage. Men in white smocks carry in files, test tubes, etc., to tables around the card file. One is dissecting an animal, another is looking through a microscope. A computer is pulled in, then several cages of rats, rabbits, and guinea pigs. Several men in white smocks stand about writing on clipboards. As general activity continues, the light slowly fades. A sinister laugh is heard but most of the scientists do not hear it. The few who do look around a bit, then forget about it and no longer appear to hear it. Even as it becomes louder none hear it. Activity continues and darkness falls. The laugh continues for a moment, then silence.

No Clockwork Orange

This sermon, based on the novel and movie *A Clockwork Orange*, was preached at an ecumenical Lenten service involving a congregation of Methodists, Presbyterians, and Roman Catholics. The lessons for the service were Psalm 8 and Luke 11:24-26. The creed was the Nicene, parts of which are reiterated in the sermon.

The parts of the sermon printed in caps could be spoken by a chorus. Music to follow the sermon could be selected from the hymn "Morning Has Broken," Carlton Young's "Saints and Sinners," and Avery and Marsh's "What Makes the Wind Blow?"

In less formal congregations, oranges might be passed among participants and they might peel and share them; in more formal situations, oranges might be handed to people as they leave.

The current movie based on an older novel, *A Clockwork Orange*, is on one level about crime in the streets.
Alex and his "droogs" take drugs and then roam the city,
 or invade lonely houses out in the suburbs,
  mugging, raping, finally killing and turning on each other.

On another level, the movie suggests *why* Alex likes drugs and violence.

Dr. Charles Rice is professor of homiletics, Drew University, Madison, New Jersey 07940.

For one thing, he is bored.
Home is flat 18A.
There are the usual ways to beat boredom:
  assembly-line labor—Alex calls it "rabbiting"—
    and "viddying the telly."
But Alex is fifteen years old.
  He finds more imaginative ways out of boredom.

Lowering over it all is Big-Brother Government, which talks a lot about stopping crime but is mainly concerned with winning the next election. Aggression feeds on boredom.
Demagogues use the very instruments of boredom to exploit fear.

But the story is, on its deepest level, about how to "cure" Alex,
  how to make him a good boy, or at least a harmless lad,
who will come home in the evening to watch telly with Mom and Dad.

Alex is caught and sent to prison, where after two years he submits to the Ludoviko Treatment, the Government's sure cure for criminality.
Strapped hand and foot to a dentist's chair,
  his eyes locked open by steel clamps,
he sits,
  surrounded by screaming stereo speakers,
    before a giant screen, on which
hour after hour, day after day, he watches, unblinking,
  goose-stepping soldiers,
    concentration camps,

bombed cities,
people being beaten, burned, raped, shot.

You might think that Alex, whose slang word for good
    is "horrorshow,"
would call for more, and ask for popcorn.
But this is more than two weeks at the movies.
He has been given injections with his breakfast, so that
    all the while
he watches the films, he is sick.
He says:

> It was very real. And when it came to the sixth or seventh
> malchik leering and smecking . . . and the devotchka creech-
> ing on the sound track like bezoomny, then I began to go
> sick. I had pains like all over and felt I could sick up and at
> the same time not sick up, and I began to feel like in distress,
> O my brothers, being fixed rigid too on this chair.

And in the background, Beethoven's Ninth Symphony
crackles and booms all the while.

The treatment works.
At the end of two weeks Alex is conditioned against
    violence.
To prove it they put him on a stage, first with a burly
    type who tweaks his nose, hard, and pushes him around,
    and then with a girl in a mini-skirt.
Alex can't touch either of them.
What is more, by accidental association—
    the doctors are indifferent to music—
his passion for Beethoven, too, has been turned
    to nausea.

Hyperexposure and hypodermics have done the job—
    they have made Alex a new man.
He retches with repulsion at the first movement toward
    violence,
        sex,
            or, as he says, "good ol' Ludwig van."
Alex stands in the spotlight.
And around the stage, as if around an altar, the doctors
    and politicians
celebrate a ritual of man-made redemption.
    "He will be your true Christian," Dr. Brodski screeches.
    "Reclamation! Joy before the angels of God."
    "It works. It really works!"

Now what about it?
Can we join in this dance around the new man?

There are those who see the human problem and its
solution in just that way.
B. F. Skinner's book has a telling title—*Beyond Freedom
    and Dignity*—and a chilling prescription for making
    better people for better living through chemistry.
Skinner's views, even for people who do not know his
name, are very gospel, full of hope for the socialization of
antisocial types.
But we shouldn't be surprised.
We are only eleven years, by the *calendar*, from 1984.

Well, we are not much given these days to dusty old
    creeds, but the
Westminster Confession of 1647 has a word:

THE WILL OF MAN IS MADE PERFECTLY AND IMMUTABLY FREE TO GOOD ALONE, IN THE STATE OF GLORY ONLY.

Now that seems to suggest, dogmatic as it is, that for as
    long as we live
we are capable of evil,
    just as we are capable of good.
To be human is to be a mixed bag.
We can, on the one hand, love and praise God,
    and we can also be cruel to ourselves and to each
        other.
Take an example that comes close to home, sex.
    To what tender purposes it can be put;
        and to what cruel perversions it can be bent.
It sometimes tears at us just because it is a truly human
    gift.
That is the way it is with us, and anyone who thinks he
    can make a good man
through chemistry,
    understands neither goodness nor humankind.
The very promise of our humanity is also our peril.
Alex, who insists on calling us "Brothers" says that when
    he listens to Beethoven he hears both
    "Devil Trombones
        and Angel Trumpets."

But they make Alex a clockwork orange.
Angel trumpets and devil trombones have no place in
    his safe new world.
He is incapable of rape,
    or tender passion.

A clockwork orange: you get the picture.
An orange, on the outside:
  alive,
     ready to burst with juice,
       bright color,
         sharp when you bite the skin,
           sweet fruit.
Inside, a clock:
  tick tock, no juices flowing,
  predictable,
    controllable,
no orange at all.

The men in white coats believe that Alex will be "your
  true Christian."
But even Alex, much later, sees through that.
The words seem nonsense to him when he first reads
  them, in a novel being written by one of his victims.
He picks the book up at random and reads:

    The attempt to impose upon man, a creature of growth and
    capable of sweetness, to ooze juicily round the bearded lips of
    God, to attempt to impose, I say, laws and conditions ap-
    propriate to a mechanical creation, against this I raise my
    swordpen.

Well, whatever Alex is, and whatever we are,
  and whatever we may become,
we are dead sure more than clockwork,
  more like oranges,
messy at times,
  but capable of growth and sweetness.

Dr. Brodski screeches about "joy in the presence of the
    angels of God" at
Alex's reclamation.
That's not quite it.
The story which ends with joy before the angels of God is
    about a son,
    who rises up,
        and returns,
to his father,
    and to a big party,
        all tearful and happy and *human*.

Now we don't wish to minimize real social problems, or
to play down what science can do to make people healthier and even happier. But this is a dangerous world, close
to 1984, in which we equate
    goodness with social conformity,
        conformity with peace,
            social engineering with salvation,
                the absence of crime with security,
                    what "works" with what is human.

Jesus tells a haunting story.

WHEN AN EVIL SPIRIT GOES OUT OF A MAN,
IT TRAVELS OVER DRY COUNTRY LOOKING
FOR A PLACE TO REST: IF IT DOESN'T FIND
ONE, IT SAYS TO ITSELF, "I WILL GO BACK TO
MY HOUSE WHICH I LEFT." SO IT GOES BACK
AND FINDS THE HOUSE CLEAN AND ALL FIXED
UP. THEN IT GOES OUT AND BRINGS SEVEN
OTHER SPIRITS EVEN WORSE THAN ITELF,
AND THEY COME AND LIVE THERE. SO THAT

MAN IS IN WORSE SHAPE, WHEN IT IS ALL
OVER, THAN HE WAS AT THE BEGINNING.

That story seems to say that badness is replaced only by
    true goodness,
not simply by altering one's outward behavior,
    by sweeping out the house;
        but by something more, like getting a new *heart*.

Alex, it is true, ceases to be a wrongdoer.
He later becomes the mere pawn of ruthless men.
But Alex's reclamation is at the cost of becoming some-
    thing other than
what God made him,
    a creature, as the psalmist has it,
        a little lower than the angels.
But, the men in white coats insist, "It works!"
"It stops crime on the streets."
The prison chaplain, however, has the last word:
    "Oh it works, all right, God help the lot of us."

Maybe that's just it: *God* helps the lot of us.
He is our strong salvation, who through the *passion* of
his Son sets us free:
    that man of like passions, who for his forty days in
    the wilderness
    heard devils and was comforted by angels;

    WHO FOR US MEN AND OUR SALVATION
        CAME DOWN FROM HEAVEN . . .
    AND WAS MADE MAN . . . .

that man like us, no clockwork orange, who when
wounded bled,
he saves *us*,
who through all the days of *our* flesh
hear both Devil Trombones and Angel Trumpets.

O ALMIGHTY GOD, WHO ALONE CANST ORDER
THE UNRULY WILLS AND AFFECTIONS OF SIN-
FUL MEN; GRANT UNTO THY PEOPLE THAT
THEY MAY LOVE THE THING WHICH THOU
COMMANDEST, AND DESIRE THAT WHICH
THOU DOST PROMISE; SO THAT AMONG THE
SUNDRY AND MANIFOLD CHANGES OF THE
WORLD, OUR HEARTS MAY SURELY THERE BE
FIXED, WHERE TRUE JOYS ARE TO BE FOUND;
THROUGH JESUS CHRIST OUR LORD. AMEN.

You Can't Nail
Jesus Down

He came to Jerusalem, sick at heart.
surveyed the scene,
and made his way to the sick heart of the city.
He entered the temple.

Wandering through the temple, talking with the crowd,
he taught
Interrupting priestly plans, he preached
provoked a question:
By what authority are you doing these things?

I will ask *you* a question, said he.
Was John baptized by heaven or by men?

Wise men they were and saw the trap he laid.
They evaded his; he then evaded theirs.

The Rev. Harold Bales is associate editor of *Tidings*, Nashville,
Tennessee 37203.

YOU CAN'T NAIL JESUS DOWN.

He stood before the council of priests and their chief.
Are you the Christ? they asked with evil intent.

If I tell you, you will not believe;
and if I ask you, you will not answer,
said he.

And they all said,
Are you the Son of God?
You say that I am,
said he.

Wily questions—slippery answers.

YOU CAN'T NAIL JESUS DOWN.

He stood before the governor
and heard the question:
Are you the King of the Jews?

You have said so,
said he,
and though in chains he slipped away again.

YOU CAN'T NAIL JESUS DOWN.

He came to his place,
place of the skull,
spread his hands and placed his feet against the wood.

A spike they drove.
A spike they drove.
A spike they drove.

YOU CAN'T NAIL JE . . . .

Darkness came,
a tomb was found,
a body bound,
a stone rolled before the door.

Jesus—
finally caught, confined,
with guards outside the door.

Then three days past,
the rock rolled back,
the body gone—
what does it mean?

Rumors fly—
some say he lives—
some claim cadaver thievery.
Who knows the truth?

What does it mean?
We preach each year about the joy of this event.
But is it true that joy is what we feel?
I myself have said:
Rejoice, the Lord is risen!
But when I rehearse the story of that week,
I cannot call my emotion joy.

173

It is something else I feel:
anxiety, bewilderment, confusion.

What does the Resurrection mean?
Jesus has escaped us.
His presence with us, Word made flesh, beguiled us.
His pain, his death, the smell of rigor mortis
confirmed our own human selves.

Now resurrection! Or thievery! Or whatever!
The result's the same—*the issue is not closed.*
He has eluded us—left us with a vaporous trail,
a shadow voice to follow.

What does Easter, resurrection, mean?
It tells us less about this man
than it tells about our selves.
It leaves us with less joy than consternation
to find

WE CAN'T NAIL JESUS DOWN.   HE HAS
   ESCAPED US!

Readers who have produced previously unpublished experimental sermons are invited to share them with the editor of this book. Should interest in this volume be sufficient, it is possible that an EXPERIMENTAL PREACHING II will be published at a later time. Copies of such sermons, which cannot be returned, should be addressed to Prof. John Killinger, Vanderbilt Divinity School, Nashville, Tennessee 37240.